markets, governance and human development

numéro coordonné par P.B. Anand, Des Gasper et Miriam Teschl

Sommaire

Markets, governance and human development

P.B. Anand, Des Gasper and Miriam Teschl*

Many analysts have described the current global economic crisis as being cataclysmic and unprecedented. Though the crisis originated with the sub-prime mortgages and risk hedging instruments in the financial sector of the United States, soon its effects have reached countries in Europe, Asia and Africa not to mention neighbours within Americas. As we write this editorial, violent protests in Greece and the loss of life of three bank workers exemplify how the tremors from the financial world translate into events with a true human cost. Many people, also in the global South have lost their jobs or fear to lose them if the economic situation does not improve. They, often the same ones, have lost their houses; others have lost their life-long savings. But this is not just an economic crisis; it is much more. First of all, one can imagine the strain that job losses and their consequences have on people themselves, their families, their children and the wider society in which they live. But then, thinking about the reasons for

* P.B. Anand: University of Bradford (UK), p.b.anand@bradford.ac.uk; D. Gasper: Institute of Social Studies, The Hague (The Netherlands), gasper@iss.nl; M. Teschl: Economics Department, University of Vienna (Austria), mt367@cam.ac.uk.

this crisis, one cannot avoid a deep feeling of rage and injustice – and maybe also of sheer astonishment.

These feelings of rage and injustice are often triggered by the fact that big investment banks and speculators who contributed to causing the crisis in the first place and were bailed out by tax payers' money continue to live unreal lives and get paid enormous bonuses. It is not quite as simple to say that some of the profits of banks should be diverted to deal with problems such as the public debt of Greece. However, the fact that Greece has been downgraded by rating agencies to "junk status" and that Greece can only borrow money from the market if she accepts to pay enormous amounts of interest – and that these payments of interest finally need to be paid by Greek people who may struggle in the next years to come to make ends meet, makes one also conclude that markets are not necessarily working for people, at least certainly not for the majority of people. In this current crisis, there are some who profit, and many who lose out. Of course, there is nothing new in the insight that those who manage badly their economy are weeded out by the market (as well as by the 'creative destruction' that Joseph Schumpeter referred to) – but how far should this go? This economic crisis also marks the need for a decisive shift from an era of "light touch regulation" to more effective regulation and an effective role for government. This is not a return to "command and control" economy or a "big-brother" government but one that requires government to be able to work more transparently and more effectively to protect the most vulnerable.

However, this crisis also raises a feeling of astonishment about the fact that so many people lived on credits that they got very cheaply but whose amount did not correspond at all to their annual earnings. How is it possible that so many people undervalued the risk they were facing by buying houses and other consumption goods on loans? To live primarily on credit cards and far above one's means seem to be part of the excesses of consumerism.

Some analysts are of the opinion that this current crisis also leads to a crisis of consumerism as it was typically understood over the last several decades of (more or less) continued economic growth. Voices proliferate that call for a change in consumption behaviour, to reduce consumption in order to avoid rapid depletion of natural resources, whether they are raw materials used in industrial processes or essential features and components of our environmental support-systems. Sustainability requires especially developed countries and their citizens to modify their lifestyles, and this not only for the sake of the current generations, but also for the sake of the future. Sustainability also requires economically ascending countries not to repeat the same mistakes that industrialised nations did some decades earlier, and to invest in greener technology in the first place. But this goes along with these countries' demand that richer nations should pay for the green development of the poorer countries. The challenge of governance in the context of international co-operation is much more than merely designing organisations to promote such co-operation. Governance involves both the processes of reaching co-operation and defining the boundaries of responsibility clearly. The Copenhagen climate conference is however an example that shows that the cooperation among different nations for the better future of all is extremely difficult to achieve and the failure to come up with important measures to reduce for example CO_2 emissions worldwide leaves attentive observers and citizens with the disquieting realization that a great deal more must be done to institute effective and purposive governance to achieve international co-operation on issues that matter.

Hence, can those three keywords – markets, governance and human development – go together? The papers that we present in this special edition, which are a selection of papers presented at a workshop with the same title, which was held at Robinson College in Cambridge last year, have all in common that they express a certain uneasiness with the current "state of being".

In the first paper, Tim Jackson, the author of the 2009 book *Prosperity without Growth* (whose French translation has just been published by De Boeck) sets the ground for the debate [1]. Continual growth on a finite planet is simply unsustainable he argues, but de-growth seems equally unappealing. The latter sounds shocking for many because we live in a world in which entrepreneurs are driven by profit and are therefore continuously looking to produce better or cheaper, or in fact merely novel, products and services. On the other hand, consumers are happily buying those products because there always is a market for novelty in households. Moreover, most goods have some symbolic importance in people's lives, for consumers express their identity through goods. But change is needed nevertheless – and this change can only happen if prosperity can be achieved by relying on capabilities that allow people to flourish, but within certain limits. There are two specific components of change. One is to develop a new ecologically literate macroeconomics. The second one requires a shift in the logic of consumerism, which means to provide alternative ways through which people can flourish, other than through the endless generation of commodities. To achieve these changes, governance is crucial. But governance itself is currently caught in a dilemma of on the one hand wanting to achieve change and on the other hand of fostering the "old" system by enhancing people's commodity consumption and thereby also the production of goods. Governance for prosperity requires that we overcome this dilemma and reconsider the idea of the social contract. It requires a shift towards values with which people can flourish without exceeding the ecological limits. According to Jackson, it is possible that we can achieve such a new value system – and we must do so.

Jean-Luc Dubois and Elena Lasida's paper argues that to steer clear of a worsening of the current crisis or the beginning of new ones, new forms of power structures and decision processes must be found that avoid increasing wealth in unequal ways. They find that some promising new avenues are opening up already. One

1. Jackson 2009, *Prosperity Without Growth*, London, Earthscan; Jackson 2010, *Prosperité Sans Croissance*, Paris, De Boeck.

concerns the various types of development project based on the principle of reciprocity that are summarised more generally under the heading of "solidarity-based economy". Amongst such projects we may count ethical funds, fair tourism, micro-credit and micro-insurance initiatives etc. At a theoretical level, the capability approach is helpful as a new way of deciding about development issues by focussing on people's functionings – what they do and are, as well as on their capabilities – what they actually can be and do. It provides a unified framework to deal with issues of poverty, vulnerability and social exclusion, which are important variables for development policies. Both aspects, theoretical and practical, are important contributions to the achievement of a socially sustainable development. That needs, of course, also to be implemented on a macro-level and not to remain simply a "bottom-up" mechanism such as solidarity-based economy currently is.

Tor Otterholt's paper proposes a more concrete form of governance: the taste approach. What he means is that it should be possible for governance to exercise an influence on the way in which people benefit from the resources they dispose. In concrete terms, this would mean to foster "cheaper" tastes and would allow achieving the same level of well-being with less means – a necessary requirement in Jackson's vision. So far, well-being policies have typically focused on the resource approach, which means to affect the amount, quality and allocation of the resources from which people benefit. The taste approach would imply that people's preferences should not be taken as exogenously given or as fixed, but rather as malleable and that governance could help to change preferences in the right direction. Otterholt shows that Happiness Economics and Libertarian Paternalism already go in this direction. But he goes beyond especially libertarian paternalism by arguing that libertarian paternalism restricts itself to "nudging" people, who are psychologically biased in certain situations to make those choices that make them better off. Otterholt's view, which is the principle of Inexpensive Preference Formation, goes further than this as it is not limited to cases of apparent irrational behaviour, but would also include cases in which people could be "nudged" in the direction of achieving their well-being on a "cheaper", including environmentally cheaper and ecologically more sustainable, basis.

Vinca Bigo calls for governance to incite a new form of responsibility. Responsibility is a crucial aspect, she believes, for sustainable development. But responsibility is often understood simply as a set of rules according to which one is supposed to act. But responsibility is more than that. It is, or includes, literally, the *ability to respond* and as such a dynamic process that needs to take account not only of particular rules, but also of contexts in which those rules should apply. Given that it is an ability, it is something that needs to be developed. Whilst most people have the capacity to be responsible, it will depend on the respective upbringing and social context whether this capacity is promoted to an ability. The responsibility Bigo is talking about is not only the following of particular rules for whose compliance one can be held accountable, it is also an empathetic process of (trying to) understand the other, whether this is the person or something else in the environment. In fact, Bigo's understanding of responsibility as ability requires a constant curiosity on the part of the person to try to understand the real nature of things. For this, the person must try to reduce any possible distortions in his or her understanding and perception of things. This is not only a personal task, but it can also be fostered by creating an environment that incites people to be responsible. Bigo suggests that such an environment is for example one in which there is a real equality between men and women in all dimensions, including child care.

Finally, Alan Kirman and Miriam Teschl analyse the claim that the economic agent is typically selfish or purely self-interested. Selfishness is of course one of those aspects that many hold responsible for the current crisis. They show that the theoretical foundation of the economic agent in economic theory is not at all limited to a purely self-interested individual. In fact, economics possesses the tools to incorporate motivations other than pure self-interest. So from which additional influences does the conventional view emerge that the economic agent is selfish? If he or she is not so "by nature", then something may turn him or her to be selfish. Kirman and Teschl analyse whether some market mechanisms are responsible for that outcome. Their conclusion is that markets do not make people "necessarily" purely self-interested. Relying on the insights of experimental economics, they comment that it has been repeatedly shown that under particular experimental conditions, such as imperfect contracts for example, people have also other-regarding preferences, which are not in line with a pure self-interested account. They argue that what seems to make the biggest difference whether or not people are behaving on the basis of other-regarding motives is whether they distribute "windfall" money or their earned money. Earned money stands of course in direct relationship with effort, a variable which many think every individual is personally responsible for. Their suggestion is that market economies put a particular weight on personal effort, and as a result promote a preoccupation with personal returns. Contributing in the background often is a simplistic conceptualisation of production, in which the role of social infrastructures and environmental systems are taken for granted and all emphasis is placed on the marginal value generated by individual effort in the taken-for-granted context. It becomes worthwhile and important to ask whether and how other values and perceptions should be fostered, that may lead to more other-regarding behaviour.

Clearly, those articles will not save the world. They will not alleviate the current crisis. Most of the content in those articles is suggestive, indicating possible ways one may or should take, on an individual and social level, in order to make things better. However, all of those articles express some unease with the current situation, call for change, and insist that decisions in the right directions have to be taken now. This insistence of academics on change may be representative or symbolic of the change that is demanded by a wider population who would be ready to change if given the right governance and the right capacities to do so. In this situation, symbolism matters. This is also the view of Law Professor Marc de Vos, who, commenting on the impact the Senate hearing of Goldman Sachs managers in the US, says that "intrinsically, there may be more symbolism involved than real issues. But symbolism matters – mindsets can alter the psychology of markets and that has an influence"[2]. We hope that by contributing to a continued debate on the possible solutions to the current crisis that affects not only the economy but our whole lifestyle and future prospects, we may influence the mindset that is going to impinge on markets and governance to foster sustainable human development.

2. Marc de Vos in an interview with BBC World Service on Tuesday 27 th of April 2010.

governance for prosperity

tim jackson*

Résumé

Cet article s'intéresse au défi de la gouvernance dans la poursuite d'une prospérité vraie et durable. Son point départ consiste en une critique de l'idée selon laquelle la prospérité doit être trouvée dans une croissance économique continue – même dans les nations les plus riches. Il met également en évidence un dilemme fondamental du débat sur la croissance. La croissance pourrait être non soutenable mais la décroissance pourrait être instable. L'article met en évidence comment ce dilemme conduit à des contradictions fondamentales, au cœur de la gouvernance moderne. L'économie basée sur la croissance condamne le gouvernement à adopter un mode spécifique de gouverner (ou « gouvernementality ») même si cela entre en conflits avec les buts sociaux et environnementaux de ce même gouvernement. Ce conflit interne explique beaucoup de la résistance viscérale que les hommes politiques et les décideurs publics expriment envers le débat sur la croissance. À l'inverse, bien sûr, se libérer de l'étouffement d'une prospérité basée sur la croissance nous offre la perspective d'une meilleure gouvernance – une nouvelle « gouvernmentality » pour une économie post-croissance.

Mots clés : *gouvernance, prospérité, croissance économique, governmentality, citoyens, consommateurs.*

Abstract

This paper addresses the challenge of governance in pursuit of a genuine and lasting prosperity. Its starting point is to critique the notion that this prosperity is to be found through continued economic growth – even in the richest nations – and to point to a profound dilemma at the heart of the growth debate. Growth may be unsustainable, but degrowth (economic contraction) is

* T. Jackson: University of Surrey, t.jackson@surrey.ac.uk.

unstable. The paper highlights the ways in which this dilemma leads to deep contradictions at the heart of modern governance. The growth-based economy locks government into a particular mode of governing (or "governmentality") even when this conflicts with government's own social or environmental goals. This internal conflict explains much of the visceral resistance which politicians and policy makers display towards the growth debate. Conversely, of course, freeing ourselves from the constrictions of growth-based prosperity simultaneously offers the prospect of better governance – a new governmentality for post-growth economics.

Keywords: governance, prosperity, economic growth, governmentality, citizens, consumers

JEL Classification: H10, P10, Q20

In the end, this economic agenda won't just require new money. It will require a new spirit of cooperation… We will be called upon to take part in a shared sacrifice and shared prosperity.
Barack Obama [2008]

INTRODUCTION

Prosperity is about things going well for us. In accordance with (*pro-* in the latin) our hopes and expectations (*speres*). Ask people what that means in practice and they'll talk spontaneously about their family, relationships, friends, security; having a decent job; feeling part of a community; participating meaningfully in society. Prosperity is about doing well in life: flourishing – in some broad sense of the word.

Income often comes surprisingly low on people's list of priorities for the good life. But it's clearly recognised as a means to an end. Higher incomes mean better choices, richer lives, an improved quality of life for us all. That at least is the conventional wisdom.

Ironically, things have never quite worked out that way. Growth has delivered its benefits, at best, unequally. A fifth of the world's population still earns just 2% of global income [UNDP 2005]. Inequality is higher in the OECD nations than it was 20 years ago [OECD 2008]. And while the rich got richer, middle-class incomes in Western countries were stagnant in real terms long before the current recession. Far from raising the living standard for those who most needed it, growth let much of the world's population down. Wealth trickled up to the lucky few.

Fairness (or the lack of it) is just one of several reasons to question the conventional formula for achieving prosperity. As the economy expands, so do the resource implications associated with it. These impacts are already unsustainable. In the last half century the global economy has expanded five times. But an estimated 60% of the world's ecosystems have been degraded [MEA 2005; UNEP 2008]. Significant scarcity in key resources – such as oil – may be less than a decade away [ITPOES 2008; IEA 2008].

A world in which things simply go on as usual is already inconceivable. But what about a world in 2050 where nine billion people all aspire to the level of affluence achieved in the OECD nations? Such an economy would need to be 15 times the size of this one by 2050 and 40 times bigger by the end of the century [Jackson 2009]. What does such an economy look like? What does it run on? Does it really offer a credible vision for a shared and lasting prosperity?

This is not to deny that poorer nations stand in urgent need of economic development. Asking China and India to curtail the rise in their living standards is never going to wash. It's worth acknowledging too all the good things growth has brought (to some of us) in the last fifty years: improved longevity, better healthcare, wider education, less drudgery, greater mobility, expanding opportunities for creativity, leisure, travel.

Of course, there's evidence too of declining trust, failing community, social recession [Rutherford 2008; Norman *et alii* 2007; Soper 2008]. But that is not the point. Rather, the point is to question whether ever-rising incomes for the already-rich are still an appropriate goal for policy in a world constrained by ecological limits. Might it not be more appropriate to curtail material demand in the richest nations and place our ambitions on some other, more satisfying, goal? Might it not be better to make room for growth, where growth really matters, to improve the living conditions of the world's poor? Might the advanced nations not aspire to a different kind of prosperity – prosperity without growth?

Since the financial crisis, there has been a resurgence of interest in this possibility [Victor 2008; Jackson 2009; Nef 2010] although the idea itself has a surprisingly long pedigree stretching back to the Limits to Growth debate in the 1970s [Daly 1972, Meadows *et alii* 1972].

The aim of this paper is twofold. Firstly, to sketch some of the parameters of the growth debate and in particular to explore what turns out to be a rather profound dilemma which sits at its heart. Secondly, to unravel the implications of the growth debate for governance.

This latter discussion is situated both in relation to the dilemma of growth and also as an element of what Foucault [1991] referred to as "governmentality" – loosely, "ways or modes of governing". In particular, I argue that the growth-based economy locks government into particular modes of governing (or attempting to govern) which are inherently conflicted. This internal conflict explains much of the visceral resistance which politicians and policy makers display towards the growth debate. Conversely, of course, freeing ourselves from the constrictions of growth-based prosperity simultaneously offers the prospect of a better governance – a new governmentality.

THE DILEMMA OF GROWTH

For the last five decades the pursuit of growth has been the single most important policy goal across the world. The global economy is almost 5 times the size it was half a century ago. If it continues to grow at the same rate that it has done, the economy will be 80 times that size by the year 2100 [Jackson 2009].

This extraordinary ramping up of global economic activity is without historical precedent. It appears to be totally at odds with our scientific knowledge of the finite resource base and the fragile ecology on which we depend for survival. And it has already been accompanied by the degradation of an estimated 60% of the world's ecosystems [UNEP 2008; Rockström *et alii* 2009]. In a very precise sense, continual growth on a finite planet is simply unsustainable.

The trouble is that doing without growth is also deeply unpalatable for all sorts of reasons. The most pressing is the structural reliance of capitalism on growth. The reasons for this are complex [Jackson 2009]. But the most important dynamic is the high emphasis placed on labour productivity. Continuous improvements in technology mean that more output can be produced for any given input of labour. But crucially this also means that fewer people are needed to produce the same goods from one year to the next.

As long as the economy expands fast enough to offset labour productivity there isn't a problem. But if the economy doesn't grow, there is a downward pressure on employment. When economic output falters, People find themselves out of a job. Firms find themselves out of business. And a government that fails to respond appropriately soon finds itself out of office. To make matters worse for government, with less spending power in the economy, public revenues fall, spending is curtailed and the ability to service public debt is diminished. A spiral of recession looms. Growth is necessary within this system just to prevent collapse.

This evidence leads to an uncomfortable and deep-seated dilemma: growth may be unsustainable, but "de-growth" [Schneider *et alii* 2010] – a managed contraction of economic output – appears at first sight to be unstable [Jackson 2009]. At first this looks like an impossibility theorem for a lasting prosperity. But ignoring the implications won't make them go away. The failure to take the dilemma of growth seriously may be the single biggest threat to sustainability that we face.

The conventional response to this dilemma is to call for "decoupling" [von Weizsäcker *et alii* 1998; Hargroves *et alii* 2010; Defra 2005]: continued economic growth with continually declining material throughput. Since efficiency is one of the things that modern capitalist economies are supposed to be good at, decoupling has a familiar logic and a clear appeal as a solution to the dilemma of growth.

Evidence for declining resource intensities (relative decoupling) is relatively easy to identify. The energy required to produce a unit of economic output declined by a third in the last thirty years, for instance. Global carbon dioxide intensity fell from around one kilo per dollar of economic activity to just under 770 grams per dollar between 1980 and 2008 [Jackson 2009].

But evidence for overall reductions in resource throughput (absolute decoupling) is virtually absent. The improvements in energy (and carbon) intensity noted above were offset by increases in the scale of economic activity over the same period. Global carbon emissions from energy use have increased by 40% since only 1990 (the Kyoto base year).

There are rising global trends in a number of other resources – a range of different metals and several non-metallic minerals for example. Worryingly, in some cases, even relative decoupling isn't happening. Resource efficiency in the use of some structural materials (iron ore, bauxite, cement) has been declining globally since 2000, as the emerging economies build up physical infrastructures, leading to *accelerating* resource throughput.

The scale of improvement required in the future is daunting. In a world of nine billion people, all aspiring to a level of income commensurate with 2% growth on the average EU income today, carbon intensities (for example) would have to fall on average by over 11% per year to stabilise the climate, 16 times faster than it has done since 1990. By 2050, the global carbon intensity would need to be only 6 grams per dollar of output, almost 130 times lower than it is today (*Figure 1*).

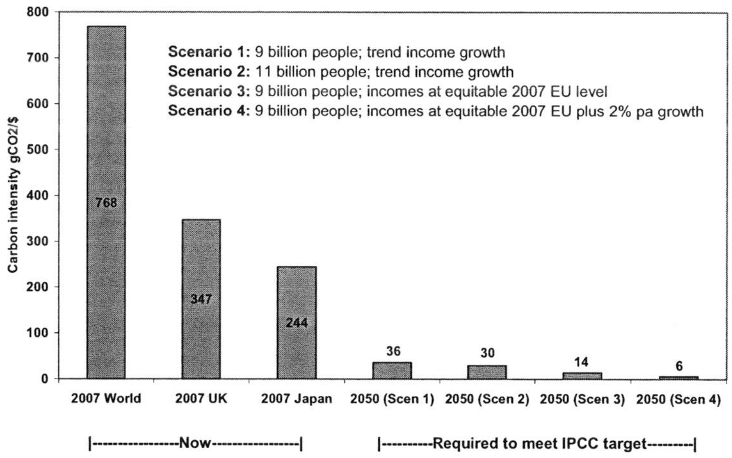

Figure 1: Carbon Intensities Now and Required to Meet 450 ppm Target [Jackson 2009]

The reality is that there is as yet no credible, socially just, ecologically sustainable scenario of continually growing incomes for a world of nine billion people. And in these circumstances, simplistic assumptions that capitalism's propensity for efficiency will allow us to stabilise the climate and protect against resource scarcity are nothing short of delusional.

THE ENGINE OF GROWTH

In fact, it seems fanciful to suppose that "deep" resource and emission cuts can be achieved without confronting the nature and structure of market economies. In particular, we're drawn inevitably towards the role of two inter-related features of modern economic life that together drive the growth dynamic [Jackson 2009; Booth 2004].

On the one hand, the profit motive stimulates a continual search by producers for newer, better or cheaper products and services. This process of "creative destruction", according to the economist Joseph Schumpeter [1934], is what drives economic growth forwards. For the individual firm, the ability to adapt and to innovate – to design, produce and market not just cheaper products but newer and more exciting ones – is vital. Firms who fail in this process risk their own survival.

But the continual production of novelty would be of little value to firms if there were no market for the consumption of novelty in households. Recognising the existence, and understanding the nature, of this demand is essential. It is intimately linked to the symbolic role that material goods play in our lives. The "language of goods" allows us to communicate with each other – most obviously about social status, but also about identity, social affiliation, and even – through giving and receiving gifts for example – about our feelings for each other [Douglas and Isherwood 1996; Jackson 2005].

Novelty plays an absolutely central role here for a variety of reasons. In particular, novelty has always carried important information about status. But it also allows us to explore our aspirations for ourselves and our family, and our dreams of the good life [Jackson 2008].

Perhaps the most telling point of all is the almost perfect fit between the continual consumption production of novelty by firms and the continuous consumption of novelty in households. The restless desire of the consumer is the perfect complement for the restless innovation of the entrepreneur. Taken together these two self-reinforcing processes are exactly what is needed to drive growth forwards.

Despite this fit, or perhaps because of it, the relentless pursuit of novelty creates an anxiety that can undermine social wellbeing. Individuals are at the mercy of social comparison. Firms must innovate or die. Institutions are skewed towards the pursuit of a materialistic consumerism. The economy itself is dependent on consumption growth for its very survival. The "iron cage of consumerism" is a system in which no one is free.

ACHIEVING CHANGE

Achieving a lasting prosperity relies on providing capabilities for people to flourish - within certain limits. Those limits are established not by us, but by the ecology and resources of a finite planet. Unbounded freedom to expand our material appetites just isn't sustainable. Change is essential.

It's possible to identify two specific components of change. The first is the need to address not just economic structure but the fundamental economics underlying this structure: to develop a new ecologically literate macro-economics. This new economic framework will have to place economic activity within ecological limits. It will need to reduce the structural reliance on relentless consumption growth and find a different mechanism to achieve underlying stability. A resilient economy – capable of resisting external shocks, maintaining people's livelihoods, and living within our ecological means – is the goal we should be aiming for here [Jackson 2009, chap. 8].

The second component of change lies in shifting the social logic of consumerism. This change has to proceed through the provision of real, credible alternatives through which people can flourish [Jackson 2008a, 2009]. And these alternatives must go beyond making basic systems of provision (in food, housing and transport, for example) more sustainable. They must also provide capabilities for people to participate fully in the life of society, without recourse to unsustainable material accumulation and unproductive status competition.

Making these changes may well be the biggest challenge ever faced by human society. Inevitably it raises the question of governance – in the broadest sense of the word. How is a shared prosperity to be achieved in a pluralistic society? How is the interest of the individual to be balanced against the common good? What are the mechanisms for achieving this balance? How is it possible to overcome the resistance of those who benefit from the unsustainability of the existing system? Is government itself one of those beneficiaries. These are some of the questions raised by this challenge. Specifically, of course, such changes raise questions about the nature and role of government itself.

Debates over the role of the state, and in particular the question of whether we need "more state" or "less state" have been fiercely fought at times and have complex roots in history [Rutherford 2008; Norman *et alii* 2007; Gough 1979]. But some striking shifts in this debate occurred as a result of the recent economic recession. The financial crisis of 2008 re-wrote the boundary between the public and the private sector and changed profoundly the landscape of 21 th Century politics.

Part-nationalisation of financial sector institutions was an almost shocking turn of events, particularly from a free-market perspective in which government is broadly seen as a distortion of the market. And yet there was little disagreement anywhere about the role of the state in the circumstances. On the contrary, the only possible response when the economy stood on the brink of failure was for governments to intervene. Even the die-hards agreed on this. "Finance is inherently unstable", acknowledged *The Economist* in the early days of the crisis. "So the state has to play a big role in making it safer by lending in a crisis in return for regulation and oversight." [Economist 2008]

Extending this basic responsibility for economic stability to the task of building a credible and ecologically robust economics seems pretty straightforward. Admittedly, it's a more complex task than anything faced in conventional macro-economics; in part because it has to depart from the well-worn formula of laissez-faire consumption growth as the basis for stability; and in part because it requires a closer attention to key ecological variables. So making progress will depend on engaging a wider community of advice than conventional approaches do. But the responsibility for taking it forwards lies unequivocally with government. As John Maynard Keynes pointed out the principal task of macroeconomics is social stability. And social stability is clearly the responsibility – perhaps the primary responsibility – of good government.

Beyond this, there are vital questions about the role of government – and the mechanisms for governance – in a much broader sense. Where, for example, does responsibility lie for the other key task identified here: redressing the social logic of consumerism? Policy-makers are (perhaps rightly) uncomfortable with the idea that they have a role in influencing people's values and aspirations. But the truth is that governments intervene constantly in the social context, whether they like to admit it or not.

A myriad different signals are sent out by the way in which education is structured, by the importance accorded to economic indicators, by public sector performance indicators, by procurement policies, by the impact of planning guidelines on public and social spaces, by the influence of wage policy on the work-life balance, by the impact of employment policy on economic mobility (and hence on family structure and stability), by the presence or absence of product standards (on durability for example), by the degree of regulation of advertising and the media, and by the support offered to community initiatives and faith groups.

In all these arenas, policy shapes and co-creates the social world [Jackson 2005, 2006]. So the idea that it is legitimate for the state to intervene in changing the social logic of consumerism is far less problematic than is often portrayed. A critical task is to identify (and correct) those aspects of this complex social structure which provide perverse incentives in favour of a materialistic individualism and undermine the potential for a shared prosperity.

At one level, this task is as old as the hills. It is, in part at least, the task of balancing individual freedoms against the common good. Governance mechanisms emerged in human society for precisely this reason. The evolutionary basis for this is beginning to be understood [Wright 1994; Sober and Wilson 1998; Jackson 2002]. Societies capable of protecting social behaviour have a better chance of survival.

The philosophical basis is provided by the concept a "social contract", an implicit arrangement between individuals and society to curb narrow individualism and support social behaviour. We hand over some of our individual freedoms. But in return we gain a certain security that our lives will be protected against the unbounded freedoms of others [O'Brien *et alii* 2009; Hayward and O'Brien 2010; Jackson 2008b].

Oxford economic historian Avner Offer [2006] provides a valuable extension of this idea in *The Challenge of Affluence*. Left to our own devices, argues Offer, individual choices tend to be irredeemably myopic. We favour today too much over tomorrow, in ways which, to an economist, appear entirely inexplicable under any rational rate of discounting of the future. Economists call this the problem of "hyperbolic" discounting. It's not unfamiliar in itself. Offer's unique contribution is to suggest that this fallibility has (or has in the past had) a social solution.

To prevent ourselves from trading away our long-term wellbeing for the sake of short-term pleasures, society has evolved a whole set of "commitment devices": social and institutional mechanisms which moderate the balance of choice away from the present and in favour of the future.

Savings accounts, marriage, norms for social behaviour, government itself in some sense: all these can be regarded as commitment devices. Mechanisms which make it a little easier for us to curtail our appetite for immediate arousal and protect our own future interests. And indeed – although this is less obvious in Offer's exposition – the interests of affected others.

The trouble is, as Offer demonstrates, affluence itself is eroding and undermining these commitment devices. The increase in family breakdown and the decline in trust have been widely noted. Parenthood itself has come under attack in developed countries. The explosion of debt, the decline of savings and the financial crisis itself reveal the erosion of economic prudence. And the hollowing out of government has left us ill-prepared to deal with this "crisis of commitment" [Offer 2006].

Strikingly, Offer places a key responsibility for this erosion on the relentless pursuit of novelty in modern society. This dynamic was identified above as a key component in the structure of modern economies. Novelty keeps us buying more stuff. Buying more stuff keeps the economy going. The end result is a society "locked in" to consumption growth by forces outside the control of individuals.

Physical infrastructure and social architecture conspire against us here. Lured by our evolutionary roots, bombarded with persuasion, and seduced by novelty: we are like children in the sweet shop, knowing that sugar is bad for us; unable to resist the temptation.

These insights are damning for the prospects that laissez-faire individualism is a sufficient governance mechanism for a lasting prosperity. Left to our own individual devices, it seems, there is not much hope that people will spontaneously behave sustainably. As evolutionary biologist Richard Dawkins [2001] has concluded, sustainability just "doesn't come naturally" to us.

GOVERNMENTALITY

It is at this point useful to draw on Michel Foucault's notion of governmentality – defined broadly as the "art of government" – or as "ways of governing" [*e.g.* Foucault 1991]. Governmentality refers in particular to the set of organised practices – mentalities, rationalities, and techniques – through which subjects are governed. It can also be thought of as the way in which governments try to produce the citizen best suited to fulfill governments' own policies [Mayhew 2004].

The importance of Foucault's work is to suggest that governments find themselves drawn into specific ways of behaving, in part as a result of their own policies. This of course is exactly what we have identified above. Social stability rests on economic stability. In a growth based economy, economic stability rests on growth. So government finds itself needing to promote economic growth just in order to maintain stability. To do this, of course, it needs citizens to be consumers. More than that, it needs them to be a particular kind of individualistic and materialistic consumer with a continued appetite for consumer novelty. And this need persists even where it conflicts with the best intentions of government to protect or enhance social and environmental goods.

Stability is, arguably, the highest of these goods. To protect it, modern governments have established a variety of practices to promote the role of the citizen as consumer. These include notions like individual freedom of choice and consumer sovereignty as well as the promotion of consumer novelty as a good in its own right. They also include the set of institutions, regulations, and market signals that co-create the culture of consumerism.

These constructions appear to us – and to government – as concrete, reified truths: "*laissez faire* policy is how markets work best"; "de-regulation is what businesses want from government"; "consumer choice is what people want". We are even led to believe that citizens are, by nature, exactly what we need them to be: individualistic, hedonistic consumers in search of the good life – cashed out in increasingly materialistic ways.

The only trouble with this – aside from its implications in the environmental crisis – is that it is patently false. In fact it's completely mistaken to suppose that human motivations are all selfish. And ridiculous to call on evolutionary justifications for this. Evolution doesn't preclude moral, social and altruistic behaviours. On the contrary, social behaviours evolved in humans precisely because they offer selective advantages to the species. All of us are torn to some extent between selfishness and altruism.

In fact, the psychologist Shalom Schwartz and his colleagues have formalised this insight into a theory of underlying human values. Using a scale that has now been tested in over 50 countries, Schwartz [2006, 1999] suggests that our values are structured around two distinct tensions in our psychological make-up (Figure 2). One is the tension between selfishness (self-enhancement, in Schwartz's scheme) and altruism (self-transcendence). The other is a tension between openness to change and conservation – or in other words between novelty and the maintenance of tradition.

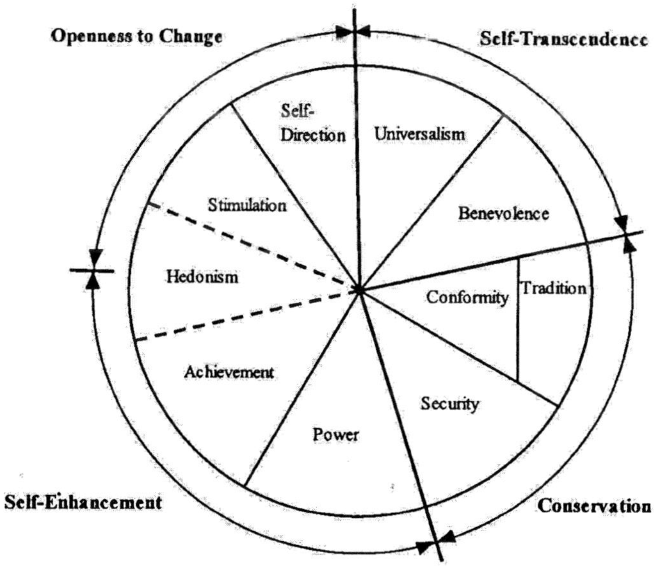

Figure 2: Schwartz's "Circumplex" of Human Values

Schwartz provided an evolutionary explanation for these tensions. As society evolved in groups, people were caught between the needs of the individual and the needs of the group. And as they struggled for survival in sometimes hostile environments, people were caught between the need to adapt and to innovate and the need for stability. In other words, both individualism and the pursuit of novelty have played an adaptive role in our common survival. But so have altruism and conservation or tradition.

The important point here is that each society strikes the balance between altruism and selfishness (and also between novelty and tradition) in different places. And where this balance is struck depends crucially on social structure. When technologies, infrastructures, institutions, social norms reward self-enhancement and novelty, then selfish sensation-seeking behaviours prevail over more considered, altruistic ones. Where social structures favour altruism and tradition, self-transcending behaviours are rewarded and selfish behaviour may even be penalised [Axelrod 1984].

This finding suggests that we must ask searching questions about the balance of the institutions that characterise modern society. Do they promote competition or cooperation? Do they reward self-serving behaviour or people who sacrifice their own gain to serve others? What signals do government, schools, the media, religious and community institutions send out to people? Which behaviours are supported by public investments and infrastructures and which are discouraged?

Increasingly, it seems, the institutions of consumer society are designed to favour a particularly materialistic individualism and to encourage the relentless pursuit of consumer novelty because this is exactly what's needed to keep the economy going. The governmentality of the consumer society demands it.

The erosion of commitment is a structural requirement for growth as well as a structural consequence of affluence. Growth calls on us to be myopic, individualistic, novelty seekers, because that's exactly what's needed to perpetuate the economic system. And at the same time, it supports us in this transition by undermining the commitment devices that support more altruistic and more conservative values.

And yet this doesn't just happen by itself. Government plays a crucial role here, precisely because it bears a responsibility for the stability of the macro-economy. The individualistic pursuit of novelty is a key requirement in consumption growth and economic stability depends on consumption growth. Little surprise then that the drift of policy is in these directions.

GOVERNANCE FOR PROSPERITY

To go back, for a moment to first principles, let us suppose here that the principal role of government is to ensure that long-term public goods are not undermined by short-term private interests. It seems ironic then, tragic even, that governments across the world – and in particular in the liberal market economies – have been so active in championing the pursuit of unbounded consumer freedoms, often elevating consumer sovereignty above social goals and actively encouraging the expansion of the market into different areas of people's lives.

It is particularly odd to see this tendency going hand in hand with the desire to protect social and ecological goals. It's notable for example that the UK, one of the most fiercely liberal market economies, has also been a vociferous champion of sustainability, social justice and climate change policy. The UK's 2005 Sustainable Development Strategy [Defra 2005] received wide-spread international praise. Its 2008 Climate Change Act [Defra 2008] is a world-leading piece of legislation.

There is a real sense here of institutional confusion. On the one hand government is bound to the pursuit of economic growth. On the other, it finds itself having to intervene to protect the common good from the incursions of the market. The state itself is deeply conflicted, striving on the one hand to encourage consumer freedoms that lead to growth and on the other to protect social goods and defend ecological limits. This tension is what historian Karl Polanyi [1942] called the "double movement" of society.

But the reason for this conflict becomes clear once we recognise the role that growth plays in macro-economic stability. It arises directly from the governmentality of the growth-based society. With a vital responsibility to protect jobs and to ensure stability, the state is bound (under current conditions) to prioritise economic growth. And it is locked into this task, even as it seeks to promote sustainability and the common good. Government itself, in other words, is caught in the dilemma of growth.

Overcoming this dilemma is absolutely vital. Because the lessons from this study make it clear that without strong leadership, change will be impossible. Individuals are too exposed to social signals and status competition. Businesses operate under market conditions. A transition from narrow self-interest to social behaviours, or from relentless novelty to a considered conservation of things that matter, can only proceed through changes in underlying structure. Changes that strengthen commitment and encourage social behaviour. And these changes require governments to act.

The trouble is that the thrust of policy over the last half century – particularly in the liberal market economies – has been going in almost exactly the opposite direction. Governments have systematically promoted materialistic individualism and encouraged the pursuit of consumer novelty. This trend has been perpetrated, mostly deliberately, under the assumption that this form of consumerism serves economic growth, protects jobs and maintains stability. And as a result, the state has become caught up in a belief that growth should trump all other policy goals. It's also encouraged into this belief of course by the pressure of lobby groups with vested interests in the prevailing system.

But this narrow pursuit of growth represents a horrible distortion of the common good and of our underlying human values. It also undermines the legitimate role of government. A state framed narrowly as the protector of market freedom in the unbounded pursuit of consumerism bears no relation to any meaningful vision of social contract. At the end of the day, the state is society's commitment device, *par excellence*, and the principal agent in protecting our shared prosperity. A new vision of governance – a new governmentality – that embraces this role is critical.

Knowing that family, community, friendship, health and so on are vital influences on prosperity, and that the ability of the individual to protect these factors is being eroded in modern society, there would appear to be a clear argument in favour of an increased role for government in this regard.

Equally, accepting that unemployment, injustice and inequality have impacts not just at the individual level but at the level of aggregate wellbeing, there would appear to be an argument in favour of government intervening to protect employment, justice and equality.

Such a role would be, in a sense, a re-invigoration of the idea of the social contract. Within such a contract, a legitimate role for government would be to strengthen and protect commitment devices which prevent myopic choice and, equally importantly, to reduce the pernicious structural impacts of economic development which increase inequality and reduce wellbeing.

Of course, such a vision requires a democratic mandate. "Political change comes from leadership and popular mobilisation. And you need both of them", argued UK Climate Change Secretary Ed Miliband in December 2008. Authoritarianism is damaging to human wellbeing in its own right [Doyal and Gough 1991; Helliwell 2003; Layard 2005]. And in any case it is unlikely to succeed in modern pluralistic societies. Governance for prosperity must engage actively with citizens both in establishing the mandate and delivering the change. But this doesn't absolve government from its own vital responsibility in ensuring a shared prosperity.

LASTING PROSPERITY

At the end of the day, prosperity goes beyond material pleasures. It transcends material concerns. It resides in the quality of our lives and in the health and happiness of our families. It is present in the strength of our relationships and our trust in the community. It is evidenced by our satisfaction at work and our sense of shared meaning and purpose. It hangs on our potential to participate fully in the life of society. Prosperity consists in our ability to flourish as human beings – within the ecological limits of a finite planet.

The challenge for our society is to create the conditions under which this is possible. It is the most urgent task of our times. In the final analysis this task challenges existing modes of governance. It calls for a new vision of governance – a new governmentality.

In this new vision, the role of government is to provide the capabilities for its citizens to flourish – within ecological limits. The analysis here suggests that, at this point in time, that responsibility entails shifting the balance of existing institutions and structures away from materialistic individualism and providing instead real opportunities for people to pursue intrinsic goals of family, friendship and community.

Unfortunately, for as long as economic stability depends on growth, this isn't going to happen. There will inevitably be a tendency for governments to support social structures that reinforce materialistic, novelty-seeking individualism. Because that's what it takes to keep the economy afloat.

But it doesn't have to be like this. Freeing the macro-economy from the structural requirement for consumption growth will simultaneously free government to play its proper role in delivering social and environmental goods and protecting long-term interests. The same goal that's vital for a sustainable economy is essential to a governance for prosperity. The conflicted state is itself a casualty of growth. And in rescuing the economy from that dilemma, it stands a chance, at least, of rescuing itself.

References

AXELROD R., 2006 [1984], *The Evolution of Cooperation*, London, Basic Books.

BOOTH D., 2004, *Hooked on Growth – economic addictions and the environment*, New York, Rowman and Littlefield.

DALY H., 1972, *The Steady State Economy*, London, W.H. Freeman and Co Ltd.

DAWKINS R., 2001, "Sustainability Does Not Come Naturally – A Darwinian Perspective on Values. The Values Platform for Sustainability Inaugural Lecture at the Royal Institution, November 14th 2001", *Fishguard, Environment Foundation.*

DEFRA, 2008, *Climate Change Act*, London, Department for Environment and Rural Affairs.

– 2005, *Securing the Future. UK Sustainable Development Strategy*, London, Department for Environment, Food and Rural Affairs.

DOUGLAS M. and ISHERWOOD B., 1996, *The World of Goods*, 2nd ed., London, Routledge.

DOYAL L. and GOUGH I., 1991, *A Theory of Human Needs*, Basingstoke, Palgrave Macmillan.

ECONOMIST, 2008, "Redesigning global finance", *The Economist leader*, November 15th, p. 13.

FOUCAULT M., 1991, "Governmentality", transl. B. Rosi revised by G. Colin, *in* G. Burchell, C. Gordon and P. Miller (eds), *The Foucault Effect: Studies in Governmentality*, Chicago, University of Chicago Press, p. 87-104.

GOUGH I., 1979, *The Political Economy of the Welfare State*, Basingstoke, Palgrave Macmillan.

HARGROVES C., VON WEIZSÄCKER E., LOVINS A., LOVINS L.H., 2010, *Factor Five*, London, Earthscan.

HAYWARD B. and O'BRIEN K., 2010, "Security of What for Whom? Rethinking social contracts in a changing climate", *in* K. O'Brien (ed), *Climate Change, Ethics, and Human Security*, Cambridge, Cambridge University Press, forthcoming.

HELLIWELL J., 2003, "How's life? Combining individual and national variables to explain subjective wellbeing", *Economic Modelling*, vol. 20, n° 2, p. 331-360.

IEA, 2008, *World Energy Outlook 2008*, Paris, International Energy Agency.

ITPOES, 2008, *The Oil Crunch: securing the UK's energy future. First report of the Industry Taskforce on Peak Oil and Energy Security*, London, ITPOES.

JACKSON T., 2009, *Prosperity without Growth – economics for a finite planet*, London, Earthscan.

– 2008a, "The Challenge of Sustainable Lifestyles", in *State of the World 2008 – Innovations for a Sustainable Economy*, Washington DC, WorldWatch Institute, chap. 4.

– 2008b, "Where is the wellbeing dividend? Nature, Structure and Consumption Inequalities", *Local Environment*, vol. 13, n° 8, p. 703-723.

– (ed.), 2006, *Earthscan Reader in Sustainable Consumption*, London, Earthscan.

– 2005, *Motivating Sustainable Consumption – a review of evidence on consumer behaviour and behavioural change*, London, SDRN.

– 2002, "Evolutionary Psychology in Ecological Economics: Consilience, Consumption and Contentment", *Ecological Economics*, vol. 41, n° 2, p. 289-303.

KASSER T., 2007, *A Vision of Prosperity. Thinkpiece for the SDC's Redefining Prosperity project*, London, SDC.

KEYNES J.M., 1930, *Economic Possibilities for our Grandchildren. Essays in Persuasion*, New York, W.W. Norton & Co.

LATOUCHE S., 2007, "De-growth: an electoral stake? ", *The International Journal of inclusive democracy*, vol. 3, n° 1, January, online at: http://www.inclusivedemocracy.org/journal/vol3/vol3_no1_Latouche_degrowth.htm

LAYARD R., 2005, *Happiness*, London, Penguin.

MAYHEW S. (ed.), 2004, *A Dictionary of Geography* ("Governmentality"), Oxford, Oxford University Press.

MEA, 2005, *Ecosystems and Human Wellbeing: Current States and Trends*, Washington DC, Island Press.

MEADOWS D., RANDERS J. and BEHRENS W.W., 1972, *The Limits to Growth. A report to the Club of Rome*, New York, Universe Books.

NEF report, 2010, *Growth isn't Possible*, London, New Economics Foundation.

NORMAN J., USSHER K. and ALEXANDER D., 2007, *From here to fraternity: perspectives on social responsibility*, London, CentreForum.

OBAMA B., 2008, Speech on "shared prosperity" delivered in Janesville (Wisconsin), February 13 th 2008, online at: http://www.barackobama.com/2008/02/13/remarks_of_senator_barack_obam_50.php

OECD, 2008, *Growing Unequal? Income Inequality and Poverty in OECD countries*, Paris, Organization for Economic Cooperation and Development.

OFFER A., 2006, *The Challenge of Affluence*, Oxford, Oxford University Press.

O'BRIEN K., HAYWARD B. and BERKES, 2009, "Rethinking Social Contracts: Building Resilience in a Changing Climate", *Ecology and Society*, forthcoming.

POLANYI K., 2002 [1942], *Great Transformation – the political and economic origins of our time*, Uckfield, Beacon Press.

ROCKSTRÖM J., STEFFEN W., NOONE K., PERSSON A., CHAPIN F.S., LAMBIN R.F., LENTON T.M., SCHEFFER M., FOLKE C., SCHELLNHUBER H.J., NYKVIST B., DE WIT C.A., HUGHES T., VAN DER LEEUW S., RODHE H., SÖRLIN S., SNYDER P.K., COSTANZA R., SVEDIN U., FALKENMARK M., KARLBERG L., CORELL R.W., FABRY V.J., HANSEN J., WALKER B., LIVERMAN D., RICHARDSON K., CRUTZEN P. and FOLEY J.A., 2009, "A safe operating space for humanity", *Nature*, n° 461, p. 472-475.

RUTHERFORD J., 2008, *Wellbeing, Economic Growth and Recession. Thinkpiece for the SDC workshop 'Living Well – within limits'*, March, London, Sustainable Development Commission, online at: http://www.sd-commission.org.uk/pages/redefining-prosperity.html

SCHNEIDER F., KALLIS G. and MARTINEZ-ALIER J., 2010, "Crisis Or Opportunity? Economic Degrowth For Social Equity And Ecological Sustainability", *Journal of Cleaner Production*, vol. 18, n° 6, p. 511-518.

SCHUMPETER J., 2008 [1934], *The Theory of Economic Development*, London, Transaction Publishers.

SCHWARTZ S., 2006, "Value orientations: Measurement, antecedents and consequences across nations", *in* R. Jowell, C. Roberts and R. Fitzgerald (eds.), *Measuring attitudes cross-nationally – lessons from the European Social Survey*, London, Sage.

– 1999, "A theory of cultural values and some implications for work", *Applied Psychology*, vol. 48, n° 1, p. 23-47.

SOBER E. and WILSON D.S., 1998, *Unto Others—The Evolution and Psychology of Unselfish Behaviour*, Cambridge, Harvard University Press.

SOPER K., 2008, *Exploring the relationship between growth and wellbeing. Thinkpiece for the SDC Seminar Living Well – within Limits*, February, London, Sustainable Development Commission, online at: http://www.sd-commission.org.uk/pages/redefining-prosperity.html

UNDP, 2005, *Human Development Report*, Oxford, Oxford University Press.

VICTOR P., 2008, *Managing without Growth – slower by design not disaster*, Cheltenham, Edward Elgar.

VON WEIZSÄCKER E., LOVINS A. and LOVINS L.H., 1998, *Factor Four: Halving Resource Use, Doubling Wealth*, London, Earthscan.

WRIGHT R., 1994, *The Moral Animal – why we are the way we are*, London, Abacus.

A NEW STYLE OF DEVELOPMENT TO DEAL WITH THE CURRENT CRISIS: SOLIDARITY-BASED ECONOMY, COLLECTIVE CAPABILITY AND SUSTAINABLE HUMAN DEVELOPMENT

JEAN-LUC DUBOIS AND ELENA LASIDA*

Résumé

Pour éviter une aggravation de la crise actuelle, comme l'apparition de nouvelles crises liées aux contraintes écologiques et inégalités socio-économiques, il devient indispensable de repenser les modes de fonctionnement des agents, les structures de pouvoir et les processus décisionnels. On peut ainsi aider à l'émergence d'un autre style de développement, d'autant plus que certains de ses constituants sont déjà à l'œuvre. Le premier, d'ordre théorique, porte sur l'approche par les capacités qui met l'accent sur les capacités d'action, effectives et potentielles, des agents, leurs libertés à choisir ce qui importe et à agir collectivement dans ce but. Le deuxième, plus opérationnel, concerne l'économie solidaire qui se réfère aux valeurs de responsabilité, d'équité et de reconnaissance pour surmonter les problèmes écologiques et sociaux actuels, en modifiant les manières d'agir et d'être des agents. Le troisième porte sur le développement durable (ou soutenable), lequel, à travers ses dimensions humaines (renforcement des capacités) et sociales (équité intra et intergénérationnelle, lutte contre la pauvreté et les inégalités, prise en compte de la vulnérabilité et de l'exclusion), offre le cadre explicatif le plus englobant. Examiner comment ces trois constituants peuvent s'articuler pour engendrer un autre style de développement est le but de cet article.

* J.-L. Dubois: Director of Research at the French Institute of Research for Development (IRD), jlucdubois@aol.com; E. Lasida: Professor at the Paris Catholic Institute, lasida.elena@neuf.fr.

Mots clés : *capacité, développement humain, responsabilité, économie solidaire, développement durable*

Abstract
To avoid a worsening of the current economic crisis, and to prevent future crises related to ecological constraints and social imbalances, there is a need to change the decision-making processes and related power structures, in order to envisage a new style of development. Indeed, three constituents of such a style are already in place. Firstly, the theoretical approach looks at the capabilities of people, at their freedom to choose what they value, and at their agency. Second, in operational terms, a solidarity-based economy regularly invents relevant solutions for overcoming changing social and ecological issues by means of a defined set of values: responsibility, equity and recognition, and the way people interact and behave. Third, sustainable development provides a global conceptual framework through its human dimension (*i.e.* the reinforcement of personal capabilities), and its social dimension (intra- and intergenerational equity, poverty and inequality traps, vulnerability and social exclusion). This paper sets out to show how these three constituents interact to generate a new style of development, which could influence the future design of public policies.
Keywords: Capability Approach, Human Development, Responsibility, Solidarity-based Economy, Sustainable Development

JEL Classification: A13, O15, P 46

INTRODUCTION

The current economic crisis has had particularly severe impacts on financially-oriented economies, where there was less organized solidarity, in economic terms, through monetary zones, and in social terms, through social protection and public services. A risk of economic failure and social unrest appears when social fragility, resulting from poverty and inequality traps, social exclusion, and vulnerability, catalyzes the impact of ecological factors such as the rising price of oil, the difficulty of accessing scarce land, etc. This is the case of the current crisis, which started in the USA and UK, then spread to Iceland and several countries in Eastern Europe, as a result of the over-indebtedness of poor households. It has also affected many other countries worldwide, where riots have occurred, as in Guadalupe and Martinique (due to their inequality traps), and in Madagascar (due to the poverty and inequality traps, and the renting of land to foreign companies).

These problems will not disappear in the near future, even if growth is resumed, because the population will still be increasing towards more than 9 billion around 2050, and ecological resources will have to be shared between ever greater numbers of people who all expect their standard of living to improve.

To avoid worsening the current crisis, or triggering new crises, it would be better to facilitate a change in the power structures and decision processes that have allowed wealth to increase in very unequal ways during recent periods of growth. This calls for a focus on the real economy, which is intended to respond to the people's needs and aspirations, to reinforce their capabilities, and to generate social interactions through their involvement in the decision-making process, which implies generating new ways of behaving and interacting with others, in order to overcome unresolved issues, such as energy needs, climate change, food production and population distribution. Each of which could lead to new crises.

In fact, this new style of development is already emerging in some places, where the constituents of its ethical foundations can already be seen [Dubois 2009a]. For instance, in theoretical terms, the "capability approach" provides new insights, especially when envisaged in an extended version. In operational terms, the "solidarity-based economy" is at the source of a series of experiments implementing such a vision. And, finally, in conceptual terms, "sustainable human development" provides an appropriate framework for dealing with the social and human dimensions of development.

These three concepts, and the way they relate to each other, will be addressed in the three parts of this paper. The first part concerns initiatives that constitute the "solidarity-based economy", that can be considered to constitute the experimental engine of this new style of development. In the second part, we discuss the "capability approach" as the theoretical foundation that can integrate responsibility and collective action, both of which are required if we are to understand the dynamics of solidarity-based economy. The third part deals with the concept of "sustainable human development" as the framework that can integrate social sustainability in a consistent way. The limitations of this threefold vision will be addressed in our concluding remarks, in which we also suggest future avenues for research in institutional and macro-analytical terms.

1. THE SOLIDARITY-BASED ECONOMY AS A SOCIAL EXPERIMENT

"Solidarity-based economy" is "*par excellence*" an area where new ways of behaving and of interacting with others are invented on the basis of the principle of reciprocity, which connects people for the purpose of achieving ends that they perceive as being fundamental for the future.

A Mirror for New Ways of Behaving and Interacting

The term "solidarity-based economy" [1] includes various specific actions which are the result of interactions within groups of people following a "principle of reciprocity" that expresses their solidarity.

This can be viewed as a particular type of economic system, where social interaction is based on the exchange of gifts (a gift and a return gift) motivated by specific feelings among the various categories of people involved in this exchange. It differs from a pure gift without hope of return, from a commercial exchange based on formal market rules (prices and quantities), and, of course, from coercion. The historian and anthropologist of economics K. Polanyi [1944] showed that this reciprocal attitude of

1. In the following pages, the term "solidarity economy" will be used to signify "solidarity-based economy" or "economy of solidarity" in order to simplify. The French translation is "économie solidaire", the Spanish and Portuguese "economia solidaria" and the German "Solidarische Ökonomie".

exchange is fundamental to the life and evolution of any society, whether traditional or developed. By referring to various anthropological instances, he showed that besides the three economic systems of the domestic economy, state redistribution, and market equilibrium, there was also a fourth system based on reciprocity rules.

The economist S.C. Kolm [2008] formalized these motivated attitudes towards partnership that occur in the various economic situations that can occur within a solidarity-based economy. Motivated individuals belonging to specific institutions agree to participate in a non-symmetrical exchange, based on their possibilities and means, the types of gifts that they can bestow on each other (goods, services, ideas…), the recognition and care they show to others, in order to achieve a joint end or common good [Laville and Cattani 2005].

Within this framework, the concept of a solidarity-based economy describes a wide range of projects with differing objectives. Some may be economic (production, consumption, trade), others social (education, health, employment, etc.), cultural (culture and identity, tradition and religious affairs), or political (participation, empowerment). The solidarity-based economy challenges the major social and environmental issues of today's world by seeking innovative solutions at the economic, social, cultural, and technological levels. Instances of such actions include ethical funds, solidarity saving schemes, fair-trade tourism, micro-credit and micro-insurance, environmental sustainability, fair trade, corporate social responsibility, the defense of indigenous or minority groups, local food provision, collective water management, etc. Indeed, worldwide there are currently thousands of such initiatives that illustrate and contribute to the emergence of a solidarity-based economy [Draperi and Fremeaux 2006].

The solidarity-based economy originally arose out of "social economy", which emerged in reaction to the injustice of capitalism at the end of the 19th century, and took the form of the cooperative movement and workers' unions (laborers, fishermen, farmers). This became quite an important force in the United Kingdom and in Germany. The concept of "social economy" continued to develop in the 20th century, and found expression in consumption cooperatives and related unions in the fields of insurance, banking, health, and housing. Over the past thirty years, it has continued to expand through the idea of solidarity-based economy, taking the formal aspects of cooperatives and mutual unions, while refining its ethical reference and innovating through setting up associations, private and public foundations, and companies of various statuses [Draperi 2005].

The solidarity-based economy is currently expanding throughout the world. Some countries stand out as pioneers, such as Brazil, which even has a State secretariat for this specialized field. It includes an increasing number of associations related to the many innovations that are emerging worldwide to solve issues in a sustainable way. It is the source of new ways of interacting to promote development, and of innovative behavior in a globalized world where different socio-cultural groups seek to achieve common goals in partnership. To respond better to people's aspirations and needs, this has led to a rethinking of existing institutions and various structures in a search for new democratic processes.

Extending Ethical References

As we have already said, the solidarity-based economy can be seen as a continuation of the momentum created by social economy, but it also goes much further in implementing the principle of reciprocity. While social economy is based on the three values of liberty (through its voluntary nature and its aim of achieving independence), equality and solidarity, by taking these values on board the solidarity-based economy has refined them to deal with the globalized context of differing socio-cultures, and the resulting multiplicity of perceptions of life, social representations and aspirations. It incorporates the fact that we are no longer in the situation of "equals acting in solidarity" envisaged by the social economy, but that we live in a globalized world confronted by a series of emergencies. Nowadays this implies a need to "act together in solidarity as equals, while remaining widely diverse". Therefore, in the context of current crises, defending a common good requires the solidarity-based economy to give priority to the common good (as a global overall interest) rather than focusing solely on the collective benefit of a specific group of equals, as the social economy usually does.

A solidarity-based economy is, therefore, more suitable for a globalized world, where people are rarely dealing with equals. It is able to address the issue of difference within a framework of fairness. In this context, the principle of reciprocity leads to specific ethical considerations, such as feeling responsible for others, searching for equity when fighting inequality, recognizing the dignity of the most vulnerable, caring for the poorest, and so on. These attitudes rely on a set of values that complement those of liberty, equality, and solidarity. Freedom needs to be accompanied by prospective responsibility; attempts to reduce inequality have to consider equity issues; and solidarity implies the recognition of others with their diverse backgrounds. Thus, responsibility, fairness and recognition, emerge as the three complementary values required by a solidarity-based economy. Let us now look at these values in greater detail.

Freedom and Responsibility

The values of freedom and equality remain fundamental values. However, what unites all solidarity-based initiatives, is the acceptance of liability for those who are at risk or vulnerable, and also for future generations, who have all too often been ignored by our existing pattern of expansion. This particular relationship between freedom and responsibility, which lies at the heart of the ethical approach to economy, has been explored by philosophers including H. Jonas [1979], with regard to the environment, and E. Levinas [1982] and P. Ricœur [2004], with regard to social interactions. Their work has revealed the need to distinguish between two forms of responsibility.

The first type of responsibility concerns the consequences of subsequent actions which are directly related to the freedom to act. This form of liability, which is known as *ex-post* or "retrospective responsibility", results from past actions. It expresses the fact of "being accountable to others" for a particular attitude. A second type of responsibility is the liability resulting from *a priori* obligations which may constrain one's freedom of action. This is known as *ex-ante* or "prospective responsibility". This liability, which is, for instance, that of parents, requires the individual voluntarily to constrain his or her own freedom in order to satisfy obligations that are viewed as having priority. It expresses the fact of "being accountable for others". This is exemplified, for instance, by a person who refrains from driving a four-wheel drive vehicle in urban areas because of feeling responsible for the fate of young children, and so not wanting to put them at risk in terms of pollution or fatal accidents.

The distinction between these prospective and retrospective dimensions of responsibility helps us to understand the current emergence in many institutions of responsible behavior in environmental or humanitarian terms. Such behavior is becoming more frequent as awareness of the serious challenges that our world is facing today increases. This is, precisely, a characteristic of the agents who are committed to a solidarity-based economy.

Equality and Fairness

The issue of prospective responsibility towards others who are most at risk, either because they are currently weak, poor or vulnerable, or because they could become so in the future, and for generations to come, calls for a rethinking of the issue of equality. One must be able "to accept some inequalities if they can benefit to the poorest and the most vulnerable" according to J. Rawls [1971] or even to ensure that reciprocity works "from each according to his ability (naturally unequal) to each according to his needs (also unequal)" according to a well-known slogan of the socialist movement popularized by Karl Marx [1875]. This means that we cannot accept, under the guise of an equal right to free movement, that some people systematically pollute the environment without raising the issue of their responsibility towards the most vulnerable. The question is then "could we live together, equal and diverse" as formulated by the sociologist A. Touraine [Touraine and Macey 2000]. It addresses the issue of fairness (or equity), which may not always be egalitarian.

This issue can only be solved by deciding which of the whole set of existing inequalities have to be opposed, because they are considered to be unfair or inefficient. However, this requires the establishment of appropriate rules of equity. Some of these rules may be universal, like those related to human rights, while others are more rooted in a particular culture and context. This generates variability: to reduce the same type of inequality, the equity rules decided by people may vary depending on their cultural context. Variability is one of the weaknesses of equity. Equity is necessary for those who want to reduce inequality while looking for fairness, but since it is originally mostly rooted in local context it does not automatically yield universal solutions. The philosopher M. Walzer [1983] also attempts to answer this question by considering various spheres of justice, each having its own criteria. Many authors have since sought to formalize the principles of such a relationship in an attempt to ensure consistency in the economic decision-making process [Clement *et alii* 2008]. This issue of connecting equity to inequality was widely debated in France in the early 1990s. What was proposed then was to do things in an appropriate order: first, to decide which inequalities will have to be reduced and, only then, to decide which criteria of fairness are relevant [Rosanvallon and Fitoussi 1994].

In a world that calls for more justice, but which also wishes to preserve the traditions and aspirations of different peoples, the notion of fairness is becoming increasingly crucial, because it relates the reduction of inequalities to the respect of freedoms. The solidarity-based economy provides responses to this issue in the form of targeted projects and initiatives.

Solidarity and Recognition

When principles of fairness are not respected, claims for recognition arise [Honneth 1992]. These claims are often based on specific cultural features shared by a group of people. A. Touraine [2005] highlighted this cultural dimension when studying social movements, and considers that it can explain differing reactions. This cultural dimension allows people to join in collective actions by recognizing what they have in common, whilst still maintaining their distinct and multiple identities [Sen 2006]. Preserving the multiple dimensions of identity also implies developing focused actions that recognize these differences. The agents of solidarity-based economy often have to deal with this dual situation: preserving multiple identities while acting collectively in a focused project. This duality is solved by recognizing the other's difference in the context of an attitude of solidarity.

Attempts to deny this cultural dimension as, for instance, in France where meritocracy is regarded as the best approach, puts children from migrant families at a disadvantage. Their cultural background and social behavior are different from those of the indigenous majority, and so they do not possess the codes that are required to succeed on an equal footing in a highly competitive environment. They are indeed legally entitled to equal access to education but, in practice, fairness and concern for their future are missing. This situation, if it is perceived as a lack of recognition of their dignity, can lead directly to unrest, as has been demonstrated by A. Honneth when considering the Paris suburb uprising in 2005.

In the specific case of disability, it may not be enough to improve the capabilities of disabled people by taking their aspirations into account. One must also perceive how they impinge on other people, in order to avoid any risk of discrimination, what are their collective intentions and what are the expectations of others towards them [Dubois and Trani 2009]? In the more general case of sustainable development we need to consider the capabilities of future generations, which supposes an awareness of the intentions of the present generations, how they envisage the future when dealing with potential crises and, of course, the feeling of responsibility that results.

2. The capability approach as a theoretical foundation

Addressing the ways people are interacting and behaving in relation to others, implies referring to development approaches that focus primarily on individuals and on their ability to conduct their own lives. The "capability approach", as proposed by economist A. Sen [1999] and philosopher M. Nussbaum [2000], fits in rather well with this view.

The Basis and Insights of the Capability Approach

A. Sen uses the concept of "capability" in a generic sense by extending the usual sense of ability/capacity into the economic sphere. This makes it possible to envisage an economy of "capable agents", rather than referring to the usual limited view of allocating resources, and managing goods and services [Sen 1985].

His analysis is expressed by a relatively simple equation. Each agent, or social actor, converts his/her endowment of material and immaterial resources (such as property, assets, rights, values, etc.) into a series of functionings, which may be either effective or potential. This is done by taking into account social and economic constraints and opportunities, as well as personal characteristics (such as gender, age, disability…). A combination of various functionings allows the individual to achieve specific objectives, such as, for example, riding a bicycle, becoming a doctor, participating in community life, and so on. This expresses the 'capability' of the agent, i.e. what he or she is effectively and potentially capable of doing and being [Bonvin and Farvaque 2008].

Here, we must distinguish between two dimensions of capability. On the one hand, the effective and observable dimension expresses what the agent is actually able to do or to be. This is a combination of achieved functionings. On the other hand, the potential or latent dimension of capability consists of those functionings that have not yet been realized, but which could be if the opportunity arose, or if the agent were to decide to realize them. Capability thus describes the full range of possibilities that an agent is, or could be, able to do and to become.

For A. Sen, capability expresses a level of "freedom to choose" among various alternative functionings available to the agent, some of which are selected and implemented, whereas others remain potentially available. In such a framework, development is intended to widen the agent's capability set or, in other words, to increase the range of freedoms that he/she can choose between. Hence, the title of Sen's book *Development as Freedom* [1999]. However, the increase in freedom must occur on an equitable basis to ensure that equality exists in the capability distribution of the various agents [Sen 1982].

The capability approach offers economists various insights. First, it allows them to focus on the agent's behavior by considering his/her set of functionings and the related aspirations, rather than remaining in the usual framework of managing goods and services (for production, consumption, trade, and allocation). Second, it provides a unified framework to deal with the issues of poverty (viewed as a deprivation of capabilities), inequality (as a result of the unequal distribution of capabilities), vulnerability (as a lack of specific capabilities), and social exclusion (as the lack of accessibility or of the capability to access to certain goods and services). Third, it relates the analysis of people's living conditions (standard of living analyses), usually conducted by economists, to that of lifestyles, which are usually the realm of sociologists. This increases the information that can be used in designing public policies.

An Extension of Responsibility and Collective Action

However, in its original form, the capability approach addresses two fundamental features of the solidarity-based economy, namely "prospective responsibility" and "collective action", but only in a very limited way. Taking these features into account implies extending the assumptions that originally underlay the capability approach.

In explicit terms, A. Sen [1999] addresses only the retrospective dimension of responsibility by considering the *a posteriori* consequences of the actions of an autonomous agent. This responsibility arises from the individual's freedom to act, and implies that freedom exists prior to responsibility. However, as we have already seen, it is prospective responsibility which is fundamental in solidarity-based economy, and this dimension of responsibility exists prior to action. Moreover, the agent's freedom of choice may be modified if he/she voluntarily restrains his/her own freedom to act, in order to fulfill what is perceived to be moral obligation.

This obviously requires a rethinking of the agent's freedom of choice by acknowledging a particular type of capability: that of the individual to voluntarily constrain his/her own freedom. For Ricœur [2004], this attitude characterizes the person, thus considered as a responsible agent. A. Sen has never taken this line, although rather paradoxically, he does recognize that responsibility towards future generations may imply reducing the capability of the current generation [Sen 2000]. Thus, the "capability of self-constraint" should be added to the capability set that human development aims at promoting on an equitable basis.

With regard to collective action, A. Sen [1999] recognizes that the social interactions between agents may generate particular capabilities, *i.e.* "socially dependent capabilities". However, he does not go any further in his analysis. As a result, he does not address the aggregative process that could explain the constitution of a collective capability through the pooling of individual and social capabilities, nor the link between collective capability and collective action [Ibrahim 2006; Ballet *et alii* 2007]. One reason why he has not done this could be the complexity that such an analytical process entails. This makes it difficult to formalize in a generic fashion, because it depends on the nature of the relationships between agents [Dubois *et alii* 2008]. A clever combination of individual and social capabilities may increase the capacity for collective action and, through collective agency, direct it towards action. In contrast, conflicts between agents can jeopardize the emergence of a collective attitude. To understand this process, the constituency of group capabilities would have to be addressed more precisely [Stewart 2005]. However, instances of such aggregative processes have already been developed for the purposes of particular experiments [Anand 2007; Sandler and Arce 2007].

3. SUSTAINABLE HUMAN DEVELOPMENT AS A CONCEPTUAL FRAMEWORK

At present the solidarity-based economy mainly focuses on innovative initiatives and projects at the micro level. Addressing the issue of development and the design of specific public policies implies expanding its scope to the meso- and macroeconomic levels. The issue is therefore how to ensure that public policies, including programs and projects, are impregnated by the founding values of the solidarity-based economy in order to promote appropriate forms of social interaction or behavior at the meso- and macroeconomic levels.

This could be done by addressing the social sustainability of human development, *i.e.* by considering how the social dimension of sustainable development relates to human development.

The Social Dimension of Sustainable Development

According to the Brundtland report, "sustainable development" is defined as development that meets the needs of the present without compromising the ability of future generations to meet their own needs [WCED 1987]. Two key ideas are inherent in this definition: the ability to meet one's needs, and intra- and intergenerational equity in the building of capabilities.

In 1992, the Rio de Janeiro Earth Summit suggested that in order to achieve Agenda 21 it was necessary to focus on three key dimensions, namely the economic, social and ecological dimensions, while seeking for appropriate sustainability conditions. The economic and ecological dimensions of sustainability are often addressed, but little has been done about the social dimension. In other words, social sustainability, and its relationship to the economic and ecological dimensions, is too often overlooked in the design of public policies.

However, taking the social dimension of sustainable development into account cannot be limited to either improving living standards, or decreasing poverty, as was stated during the 2002 Johannesburg Summit. The Brundtland report implies that we need both to improve capability within the present generation, and to ensure capability equity between generations.

A. Sen, for his part, has emphasized that sustainable development must improve the capabilities of the present generation without compromising any enhancement in the capabilities of future generations [Sen 2000]. This establishes a fundamental relationship between the equitable strengthening of capabilities, and development that is sustainable in social terms. Such a vision is promoted by the United Nations Development Program through its annual reports on human development [UNDP 2005], and through the corresponding national reports that focus on specific issues.

It is no longer only a question of sharing or redistributing resources that are becoming scarce, such as oil, drinking water, fish, timber, etc., but also of ensuring a more equitable distribution of human capabilities, making it feasible to live together despite the tensions that are emerging from the current crises related to energy, food, climate, natural biodiversity.

The main concern of the social dimension of sustainable development is to avoid implementing public policies – whether economic, social or environmental – that could have the unintended consequence of generating social dysfunction. This implies the need to look at the social interactions and networks that connect the various agents in order to fight extreme poverty and exclusion, while ensuring that access to social services, the constitution of human and social capital, and the improvement of capability are not jeopardized for the current generation or for those to come [Dubois 2009b].

Social vs. *Societal*

In such a context, one may notice that the word "social" used to describe the corresponding dimension of sustainable development frequently covers the dual aspects of social and "societal".

"Social" concerns mainly those social sectors such as health, education, nutrition, employment and social affairs. "Social sustainability" focuses on the sustainability within these sectors by considering, for instance, the prevalence of HIV/AIDS [Dubois 2003], the dropout rate from education, or the level of (un)employment and so on.

In contrast, "societal" development addresses the internal quality of the society, i.e. the nature and intensity of the social interactions between the various agents. It affects all the social ties that people form amongst themselves that allow reciprocity, partnership, solidarity, social cohesion, and trust to develop. Destruction of these social ties can lead to divisions and social exclusion, and even famine or genocide. This has crucial consequences for the economic decision-making process, and for the capability of agents to act and create individually or collectively.

To acknowledge the growing role of these social and societal interactions in a globalized world calls for a clear distinction to be drawn between them. This is why we prefer to speak of "socially-sustainable development" rather than "sustainable social development" when addressing the issue of social sustainability. The term "socially sustainable" conveys the dynamic nature of the innovation that arises from social interactions within a given society much better than simply describing development as being both "social" and "sustainable".

Ensuring the Social Sustainability of Public Policies

The implementation of development strategies combines public policies in various areas such as infrastructures, agriculture, industry, transport, health, education, social affairs, culture, etc.

If policies are inappropriate to local conditions they can have perverse effects, leading to situations of social exclusion, increasing the vulnerability of certain populations, and generating new forms of inequality. By triggering frustration and feelings of injustice, they can lead to a loss of social cohesion. Economists usually refer to "social externalities", however, these "externalities" can have serious consequences, leading to irreversible human costs such as forced migration, suicide and armed conflicts.

Development that is intended to be socially sustainable must avoid such situations by taking the widest view possible of the social situation, and making an assessment of the likely social impact of intended policy measures before they are implemented. In practice, this means seeking conditions that will ensure social sustainability. These conditions may or may not be related to the economic and ecological dimensions. This requires introducing specific methods to evaluate the retrospective and prospective consequences of the planned actions, and advocating prudential and precautionary social principles [Ballet *et alii* 2005]. These principles should ensure that the human costs are minimized, and that compensation is awarded in the event of things going wrong. This stems naturally from the prospective responsibility of the agents, especially those responsible for deciding public policies [Mahieu 2008a].

It follows that any development strategy intended to be socially sustainable will have to rethink the design of public policies, and conceive them both "with the public" and "for the public". Such a bottom-up approach allows social stakeholders to participate, and express their views. However, this raises a number of methodological issues related to the definition of capabilities, the determination of ethical rules, and the establishment of priorities and standards for the quality of life expected. Even when development is not conceived as a top-down process, the State and the institutions related to it still have a key role to play as the global coordinator. This approach makes it possible to invent new ways of managing the relationship between the beneficiaries and actors of development.

Within this framework, the solidarity-based economy is naturally part of this bottom-up dynamism, because it is rooted in social networks when implementing locally-identified projects. These projects constitute a wide range of innovative experiments that can be regarded as the experimental part of socially-sustainable development.

Back to the Human Development Framework

Even if solidarity-based economics effectively reflects a new style of development at the project level, or even at the level of public policy programs, the issue remains of how to make this bottom-up dynamism extend to the point where it affects the overall design of macroeconomic development strategies.

There is an intermediate stage, however, that involves the implementation of decentralized policies; this mainly concerns the management of public utilities such as water or electricity. In this context, institutional changes have already provided some interesting approaches by moving first from public to private management, and then to decentralized management involving the various stakeholders [Makkaoui and Dubois 2010]. However, this improvement is still insufficient, because it still does not provide the overall framework that is required to manage the whole economy in a solidarity-based way.

Sustainable human development resolves this issue by providing the framework required. The project initiated in 1990 by the first Human Development Report, under the leadership of Mahbub ul Haq [1995] with conceptual backing from A. Sen, was intended to promote a type of human development that will equitably reinforce people's freedoms to choose, on an individual and collective basis, the type of life they wish to live. In this context, many policy guidelines have been designed and implemented that focus on areas as diverse as education, health, gender, disability, poverty, consumption, social capital… [Reboud 2006]. Numerous human development reports have been compiled on these topics at the global and national levels.

By introducing environmental issues and interactions into the social and economic dimensions, the Rio de Janeiro Earth Summit extended this conceptual framework to the sustainability of development. The notion of "sustainable human development" opens the way to new opportunities for analyses that include areas such as human poverty, human security, environment, etc.

When addressing the issue of social sustainability through an analysis of the quality of social interactions, it is useful, as we explained above, to differentiate between the concepts of "socially sustainable" (related to societal dimension) and "sustainable social" (related to social sectors). One may wonder whether a similar attitude could not be adopted when dealing with the issue of "human sustainability", by looking for a "humanly" sustainable development that will take into account the human costs of development and the definition of the subject who bears these costs individually or through his/her interactive social network [Mahieu 2008b]. Obviously, this would open the door to new types of analysis of how the various human dimensions interact at the global and national levels.

CONCLUSION

A new style of development is already on its way, in both experimental and theoretical terms, through the various economic approaches that deal with human interactions and behavior. First, it is integrated into a socially-sustainable view of development based on the person's "capability for responsibility". Second, it is regularly attempted in the solidarity-based economy, which remains a source of innovation in the ways of interacting and behaving with others, when confronted with development issues. And, finally, it forms part of the theoretical basis of the capabilities approach, which considers people's ability to lead the type of life they want, using their own agency to relate with others.

This makes it possible to integrate into the economic analysis various forms of cooperation, exchange and substitution, which are related to the reciprocal considerations and attitudes that the agents may have when confronted by diverse development objectives. To what extent such bottom-up dynamism will be sufficient to lead to a rethinking of development strategies by integrating the values promoted by solidarity-based economy is still a key question. More specifically, will this dynamism grow sufficiently to penetrate all levels of the decision-making process, whether micro-initiatives, meso-institutions or macro-economics, in order to change the overall design of development strategies? It is too early to tell.

Nevertheless, sustainable human development clearly offers an opportunity to build an appropriate framework that is able to envisage the whole economy in the light of the solidarity set of new values. However, further research is called for on the subject of development and on the institutions and economic processes that can promote this new style of development. For the subject and his/her social interaction, it may be useful to return to phenomenology as a philosophical basis in attempting to extend the concept of "agent" to the person, by including prospective responsibility, intentionality and the meaning given to things [Giovanola 2005]. Concerning the role of institutions, in-depth reflection is still required about the role of meso-institutional decision levels in the constitution of individual and collective capabilities. This could be addressed in several ways, for instance either through the action of individuals as constituents of the society [de Munck and Zimmermann 2008], or as the direct result of institutional capabilities of local communities or the State [Sassen 2007].

REFERENCES

ANAND P.B., 2007, "Capability, sustainability, and collective action: an examination of a river water dispute", *Journal of Human Development*, vol. 8, n° 1, p. 109-132.

BALLET J., DUBOIS J.-L. and MAHIEU F.-R., 2007, "Responsibility for Each Other's Freedom: Agency as the Source of Collective Capability", *Journal of Human Development*, vol. 8, n° 7, p. 185-201.

– 2005, *L'autre développement: le développement socialement soutenable*, Paris, L'Harmattan.

BONVIN J.-M. and FARVAQUE N., 2008, *Amartya Sen: une politique de la liberté*, Paris, Michalon.

CLEMENT V., LE CLAINCHE C. and SERRA D., 2008, *Théorie de la justice et de l'équité*, Paris, Economica.

DE MUNCK J. and ZIMMERMANN B., 2008, *La liberté au prisme des capacités: A. Sen au-delà du libéralisme*, Paris, EHESS.

DRAPERI J.-F., 2005, *Making Another World Possible: Social economy, cooperatives and sustainable development*, Paris, Presses de l'Économie Sociale.

— and FRÉMEAUX Ph., 2006, *L'économie sociale de A à Z*, Paris, Alternatives économiques pratique, n° 22.

DUBOIS J.-L., 2009a, "La notion de 'style' est-elle transposable au développement durable", *Transversalités*, n° 109, janvier-mars, p. 35-53.

– 2009b, "Searching for a Socially Sustainable Development: Conceptual and Methodological Issues", *in* R. Gotoh and P. Dumouchel (eds.), *Against Injustice: The New Economics of Amartya Sen*, Cambridge, Cambridge University Press, p. 75-294.

– 2003, "Food Security, Vulnerability and Social Sustainability", *Cahiers de l'IFAS*, n° 3, Johannesburg, p. 15-21.

— BAKHSHI P., BOUILLET A.-S. and DURAY-SOUNDROU C., 2008, *Repenser l'action collective: une approche par les capabilités*, Paris, Réseau IMPACT-L'Harmattan.

— and TRANI J.-F., 2009, "Extending the Capability Paradigm to Address the Complexity of Disability", *ALTER, European Journal of Disability Research*, vol. 3, Issue 3, July-Septembre, p. 192-218.

GIOVANOLA B., 2005, "Personhood and Human Richness: Good and Happiness in the Capability Approach and Beyond", *Review of Social Economy*, vol. LXIII, n° 2, p. 249-267.

HAQ M. ul, 1995, *Reflections on Human Development*, Oxford, Oxford University Press.

HONNETH A., 1992, *The Struggle for Recognition: The Moral Grammar of Social Conflicts*, Cambridge, Polity Press.

IBRAHIM S., 2006, "From Individual to Collective Capabilities: The Capability Approach as a Conceptual Framework for Self-help", *Journal of Human Development*, vol. 7, n° 3, p. 397-416.

JONAS H., 1979, *The Imperative of Responsibility. In Search of an Ethics for the Technological Age*, Chicago, University of Chicago Press (transl. from *Das Prinzip Verantwortung*, Frankfurt, Insel Verlag, 1979).

KOLM S.-C., 2008, *Reciprocity: An economics of Social Relations*, Cambridge, Cambridge University Press.

LAVILLE J.-L. and CATTANI A.D., 2005, *Le dictionnaire de l'autre économie*, Paris, Gallimard.

LEVINAS E., 1982, *Ethics and Infinity*, Pittsburgh, Duquesne University Press (transl. from *Éthique et Infini*, Paris, Fayard, 1982).

MAHIEU F.-R., 2008a, *Responsabilité et crimes économiques*, Paris, L'Harmattan.

– 2008b, "Face aux sacrifices humains: un développement humainement soutenable", *Revue Tiers-Monde*, n° 195, p. 495-507.

MAKKAOUI R. and DUBOIS J.-L., 2010, "Nouvelles formes de gouvernance dans le domaine de l'eau. Apports et limites de la coopération décentralisée dans les pays en développement", *Développement Durable et Territoires*, vol. 1, n° 1, online at: http://developpementdurable.revue.org

MARX K., 1875, *Critique of the Gotha Program*, Rockville, Wildside Press.

NUSSBAUM M.C., 2000, *Women and Human Development: The Capabilities Approach*, Cambridge, Cambridge University Press.

POLANYI K., 2001 [1944], *The Great Transformation: The political and Economic Origins of Our Times*, Boston, Beacon Press.

RAWLS J., 1971, *A Theory of Justice*, Cambridge, Harvard University Press.

REBOUD V., 2006, *A. Sen: Un économiste du développement?*, Paris, AFD.

RICŒUR P., 2005, *The Course of Recognition*, Cambridge, Harvard University Press (transl. from *Parcours de la reconnaissance*, Paris, Stock, 2004).

ROSANVALLON P. and Fitoussi J.-P., 1994, *Le Nouvel âge des inégalités*, Paris, Seuil.

SANDLER T. and ARCE D., 2007, "New Face of Public Assistance: Public Goods and Changing Ethics", *Journal of International Development*, vol. 19, p. 527-544.

SASSEN S., 2007, *A Sociology of Globalisation*, New York, W.W. Norton & Company.

SEN A.K., 2006, *Identity and Violence. The Illusion of Destiny*, London, Allen Lane.

– 2000, "The Ends and Means of Sustainability", Keynote Address at the International Conference on *Transition to Sustainability*, 15 May 2000, Tokyo.

– 1999, *Development as Freedom*, New York, Knopf.

– 1985, *Commodities and Capabilities*, Amsterdam, Elsevier.

– 1982, "Equality of What? ", in *Choice, Welfare and Measurement*, Oxford, Blackwell, reed. Harvard University Press, p. 353-369.

STEWART F., 2005, "Groups and Capabilities", *Journal of Human Development*, vol. 6, p. 185-204.

TOURAINE A., 2007, *A New Paradigm for Understanding today's World*, Cambridge, Polity (transl. from *Un nouveau paradigme. Pour comprendre le monde d'aujourd'hui*, Paris, Fayard, 2005).

— and MACEY D., 2000, "Can We Live Together? Equality and Difference", Palo Alto, Standford University Press (transl. from *Pourrons-nous vivre ensemble? Égaux et différents*, Paris, Fayard, 1997).

UNDP, 2005, *The Human Development Report 1990-2004: 15 Years of Publication*, Statistical Data Base, New York, United Nations Development Program.

WALZER M., 1983, *Spheres of Justice*, Oxford, Blackwell.

WCED (World Commission on Environment and Development), 1987, *Our Common Future*, Oxford, Oxford University Press.

"The taste approach" Governance beyond Libertarian Paternalism

Tor Otterholt*

Résumé

Le bien-être peut être promu de deux façons: en premier lieu, en changeant la quantité, la qualité et l'allocation des paniers de consommation (l'approche par les ressources) et en second lieu en influençant la façon selon laquelle les personnes profitent de leurs biens (l'approche par les goûts). La première approche est un ingrédient classique de l'analyse économique, alors que la seconde n'est pas encore conventionnellement intégrée dans l'analyse économique. L'article s'interroge sur le pourquoi de cette asymétrie en identifiant les gains de l'approche par les goûts. Si l'approche par les goûts est mise en œuvre avec succès, elle pourrait permettre aux individus d'augmenter leur bien-être mais aussi donner des solutions à certains enjeux actuels comme le développement soutenable ou la justice mondiale.

L'auteur argumente que des développements récents comme l'économie du bonheur (Happiness Economics, *HE*) *et le paternalisne libertarien* (Libertarian Paternalism, *LP*) *peuvent tous deux être considérés comme des cas particuliers de l'approche par les ressources. Un troisième cas est également identifié: la formation de préférences peu coûteuses* (Inexpensive

* This article is based on a presentation at the Workshop "Markets, Governance and Human Development", Tobinson College, Cambridge, where I received insightful comments. Thanks also for very useful textual comments firstly from Carl Henrik Knutsen, Miriam Teschl and an anonymous referee from RPE, but also from Bjørn Høyland, Tommy Knutsen and Vegard Sørebø. Thanks for fruitful discussions firstly with G.A. Cohen, Teun Dekker, Jakob Elster, Omar Kahn, Raino Malnes and Adam Swift, and also with Nils August Andresen, Geir Asheim, Hilde Bojer, Robert Huseby and Torbjörn Tännsjö. T. Otterholt: University of Oslo, Institute for Political Science, The Ethics Programme, CSMN, tor.otterholt@stv.uio.no.

Preference Formation, *IPF*). *Alors que le LP suggère qu'une « architecture » des choix devrait être mise en œuvre lorsque la rationalité échoue, IPF avance que la gouvernance dans certaines situations pourrait également améliorer les choix, même en l'absence d'échec de la rationalité.*
Mots clés : *goûts coûteux, paternalisme libertarien, économie du bonheur et du bien-être, développement durable, bien-être, formation des préférences*

Abstract
Well-being can be promoted in two ways. Firstly, by affecting the quantity, quality and allocation of bundles of consumption (the Resource Approach), and secondly, by influencing how people benefit from their goods (the Taste Approach). Whereas the former is considered an ingredient of economic analysis, the latter has conventionally not been included in that field. By identifying the gain the Taste Approach might yield, the article questions whether this asymmetry is justified. If successfully exercised, the Taste Approach might not only enable people to raise their well-being, but also provide solutions to a number of issues such as sustainable development and global justice.
The author argues that recently developed accounts such as *Happiness Economics* (HE) and *Libertarian Paternalism* (LP) both can be considered specifications of the Taste Approach. Furthermore a third specification is identified: *Inexpensive Preference Formation* (IPF). Whereas LP suggests that choice architecture should be exercised when rationality fails, IPF holds that governance in certain instances should improve choices also in absence of no such failure.
Keywords: Expensive tastes, Libertarian Paternalism, Happiness and Welfare Economics, sustainable development, well-being, preference formation

JEL Classification: B40, D63, I30

INTRODUCTION

Some people are more efficient than others in how they benefit from their bundles of goods. In philosophy this fact has been particularly addressed in the "Equality of What debate" over the last decades. There, these differences have been defined in terms of the expensiveness of tastes: "A person's tastes are expensive in the required sense if and only if [...] they are such that it costs more to provide that person than it costs to provide others with given levels of satisfaction or fulfillment" [1] [Cohen 2004].

Due to different understandings of the ideal of justice, egalitarians have disagreed about whether expensive tastes should be considered a handicap for which people should be economically compensated. Instead of pursuing this discussion, I will examine the attractiveness of another strategy for tackling expensive tastes: lowering them.

The motivation for raising this discussion stems from the following train of thought: Human well-being matters, and its enhancement should be one of the aims of policy making. Well-being can be promoted in two ways: Firstly, by affecting the amount, quality and allocation of the resources from which people benefit ("The Resource Approach"); and secondly, by exercising influence on the way in which people benefit from the resources that they dispose ("The Taste Approach"). The Resource Approach is conventionally considered a necessary ingredient of good governance, and is a central component in both Macro and Micro Economics. The Taste Approach, on the other hand, has for long not been integrated in these fields, and has consequently played a marginal role in areas of governance dominated by economists. Instead, preferences have been mainly considered exogenous and beyond governmental control and not as entities influenced by institutional design.

Insofar as taste formation could be controlled by policies, policy makers would gain an extra means to reach ends. However, utilization of this means would violate two standard assumptions of Welfare Economics: firstly, the empirical assumption of stable preferences; and secondly, the normative assumptions of consumer sovereignty: the economic agent should be considered the best judge of his own well-being. Thus, the question of whether utilization of this means is sensible requires both empirical investigation and normative discussion. Whereas relevant empirical research in Behavioral Economics and related fields like

1. As emphasized by Cohen [2004] the "technical" definition of "expensive taste" violates the ordinary meaning of the phrase.

neuroscience and evolutionary psychology has escalated rapidly the last decades, the normative discussion has not sufficiently taken place in mainstream Political Philosophy. This neglect can be exemplified by the expensive taste debate in luck egalitarian literature [Cohen 1989, 2004; Dworkin 2000]. It is striking that over thirty years it has been debated whether society is obliged to provide more to those with expensive tastes than to others, without discussing the alternative strategy of handling expensive tastes: cultivating less expensive ones.

Here, I investigate whether the asymmetry between the Taste and the Resource Approach is justified. If not, then to what extent and under which circumstances should promotion of well-being by the Taste Approach be considered a constituent of good governance? Approaching these questions, I will not only examine normative premises of the Taste Approach, but also discuss methodological positions associated by various specifications of this approach. Firstly, however, I will in section 1.1 present necessary terminology and clarify basic intuitions behind and attractive features of the Taste Approach. In Section 2, I examine two recently developed accounts which I consider as specifications of the Taste Approach: *Happiness Economics* and *Libertarian Paternalism* (LP). In Section 3, I construct and discuss a third specification of the Taste Approach, *Inexpensive Preference Formation*, which extends beyond LP.

1. THE BASIC IDEA

Presenting the Taste Approach, I use the terminology of tastes and their costs [2]. Flipping, and slightly paraphrasing, Cohen's aforementioned definition of expensive tastes, we get that a person has low taste costs if and only if he needs less income than others

2. The "Equality of What" literature tends to discuss tastes in terms of their price. I, however, distinguish between high cost- and low cost tastes. For a discussion on terminology, see Otterholt [2005].

in order to reach some level of well-being[3]. The relationship (r) between Well-being (W), Costs of Tastes (C) and Income (I) can then be expressed by the following equations:

(r): W = I/C From (r) follows that: (r*): C = I/W

By increasing W by means of the Resource Approach, the state affects I. By increasing W by means of the Taste Approach, the state reduces C.

1.1. *Four attractive features*

Given that the global pool of resources is finite, the Taste Approach has several appealing features. Firstly, whereas the pool of resources of planet earth is not endless, it is not evident that potential level of W of its population has a corresponding upper limit. The Taste Approach is thus attractive insofar as well-being is good and worth pursuing, *ceteris paribus*. Secondly, the Taste Approach has the virtue that it could be compatible with enhancement of W in ways which does not need to violate the principle of sustainable development. By raising W by reducing C, W could be promoted without increasing the consumption of non-renewable resources and emissions of greenhouse gases. Thirdly, Taste Approach policies could be helpful in facilitating the abolishment of global poverty. In theory, W could be increased in non-affluent countries without a decrease in W in affluent countries, firstly by reducing C in non-affluent countries or alternatively/additionally by reducing C in both affluent countries and subsequently transfer resources to the non-affluent. The same principle could apply nationally, locally and intergenerationally.

Fourthly, the Taste Approach offers a framework which considers quality, quantity and allocation of human and material resources as variables that are functions of people's propensity,

3. Other factors than income (such as the presence of common goods) that the Resource Approach could be concerned with might also affect W. Presently, presenting the Taste and not the Resource Approach, I here for sake of simplicity refer to all these factors as income. This simplification does not mean that what is neglected is not considered as important.

firstly; to choose productive and well-being enhancing activities instead of unproductive and harmful ones, and secondly; their ability to enjoy these activities. The former factor, which determine the opportunity costs of people's tastes, I denote C_0 and the latter factor I denote C_E. The assumed relations between Taste Approach policies and its potential direct and indirect targets; C_0, C_E, I, C_R (determined by a person's conversion rate between I and W) and finally, W, are identified below in *Figure 1*.

As it would be sensible to assess the impact of the Taste Approach suggested by this figure on aggregated level, C should not only be defined individually, but also collectively. Thus, C is low in a *collective sense* if and only if society needs less income than others in order to reach some level of W on aggregated level. A potentially efficient way of reducing C in its collective sense, would be to design Taste Approach policies that promote formation of positive externality producing preferences and restrict formation of negative externality producing preferences [4].

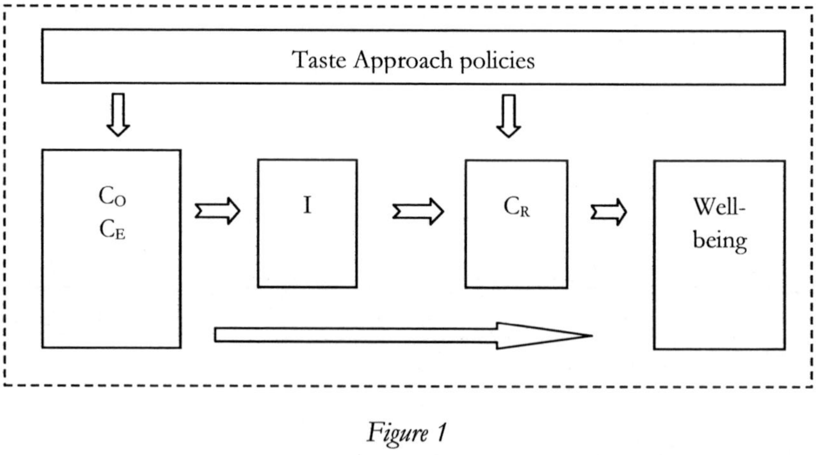

Figure 1

In sum, by considering the various specifications of C just identified as targets for policies, the Taste Approach has the virtue

4. An interesting group of examples would be problems related to collective action. By change people's pay-off structure through preference manipulation the Taste Approach avoid problems collective action challenges such as the Dilemma and the Tragedy of the Commons from emerging [Olson 1971].

that a number of social problems appearing irresolvable given people's current nature and constitution seem to be avoidable.

1.2. *Normative framework*

Despite, the attractive features of the Taste Approach, it is an open question, firstly whether reduction of C is practically feasible, and secondly, whether it is normatively appealing. In the present context, practical hindrances apply on two levels: those who would use the Taste Approach and those affected by it. The latter level includes genetic and social factors restricting the extent to which C can be institutionally influenced[5]. Feasibility concerns on the former level includes the question of whether governance can be organized in ways which ensure that governors can be trusted with power the Taste Approach would assign to them.

In this article, I pursue these aspects only briefly. Instead, I primarily examine the normative appeal of the Taste Approach, and some methodological positions with which these premises are associated. The former matter hinges on five questions:

(1) Which values are being promoted when the state reduces C?
(2) How should these values be understood?
(3) Which values are violated when the state reduces C?
(4) How should these values be understood?
(5) What is the relationship between the values identified in (1), (2), (3) and (4)?

Presently, I focus on (1) and (2), but also the remaining three will be illuminated. Below, I make some preliminary notes on all five. As far as (1) and (2) are concerned, it follows from (r) that W increases when C falls. In principle, the Taste Approach could be consistent with any conception of W: mental state-, desire fulfillment-, substantive good- and capability theories [Griffin 1986][6]. Here, I focus on the two first ones[7].

5. In principle, the Taste Approach could involve both social and genetic engineering.

6. Here, the literature uses different names for nearly identical theories. For a presently relevant discussion see Otterholt [2005, p. 20-28].

According to mental state theories, W is determined by the quality of a person's mental state. These theories were long discredited by Nozick's thought experiment, the "Experience machine" [1974, p. 42] which suggests we do not (only) care about our experiences, but also about control and authenticity. Note, that the example only suggests that experiences is not the *only* that is important to us. The appearance of one black swan doesn't prove that there are no white ones.

According to desire theories, W consists in desire fulfillment[8]. Although desires are mental states, desire theories judge W not according to mental states, but according to the state of the world [Griffin 1986, p. 6] Thus, they escape Nozick's challenge [*ibid.*]. By discarding people's consciousness as a determinant of well-being, desire theories encounter other problems. For instance, it may seem implausible that the fulfillment of a desire makes a person better off if she is unaware of it [*ibid.*].

Let me now turn to make some preliminary notes concerning (3), (4) and (5). Assume that utilitarians were right that the overarching principle for governance is to maximize utility. Then, (3) and (4), would have no relevance, and (5) will be answered merely by reference to (1) and (2). Then, the question of whether the Resource or the Taste Approach should be exercised would simply be matter of efficiency.

Insisting that W matters, the Taste Approach takes the utilitarian perspective as point of departure. However, I do not assume that the classic utilitarian perspective on C necessarily provides the whole picture. Instead, (3) and (4) are taken into account. An important question then, is whether potential candidates of (3), such as rights and autonomy should be considered as side constraints or whether they could be traded off against gain in W [Nozick 1974, p. 31]. I return to this question in 3.2.

7. *Ibid.* [p. 24-27] shows how the Taste Approach also could be combined with substantive good theories.

8. As Rozati notices, it is common practice that the terms preferences and desires are used interchangeably in the literature on well-being [2006, p. 33]. I will here follow that practice and consider the value of preference satisfaction and desire fulfilment as identical.

2. HAPPINESS ECONOMICS AND LIBERTARIAN PATERNALISM

During the preceding decade, several accounts challenged the assumption that preferences should be taken as given variables. Below, I show that two of them, Libertarian Paternalism (LP) and Happiness Economics (HE), both can be considered specifications of the Taste Approach and examine their pros and cons with particular emphasis on their conceptions of W and their methodological merits.

2.1. *Happiness Economics and Taste Formation*

In 1974 Easterlin provided data suggesting that happiness at the national level does not increase with income, once basic needs are fulfilled (1974). Several later studies have supported this "paradox of affluence" [Oswald 1997; Frey and Stutzer 2002]. Others have questioned it [Hellevik 2008; Stevenson and Wolfers 2008]. A common denominator for all these studies, however, is that national happiness does not hinge solely on income. In mainstream Macro and Micro Economics this insight has mainly served as background knowledge, exercising marginal influence on the methodological framework of standard approaches.

Recently, however, happiness studies have been the object of considerable attention. This trend escalated particularly after the publication of Layard [2005] [9]. Layard asserts that Public Economics is on the right track when "(p)olicy instruments are set so as to maximize the sum of (cardinal) utilities" [2006, p. 31], but by referring to research from other social sciences that indicate that current economic and community policies affect happiness negatively through their effects firstly on social mobility and secondly on norms, he argues that by not accounting for these mechanisms conventional approaches fail to promote happiness [2006, p. 30-33].

Attacking the assumption that tastes should be considered as given, Layard asserts the assumption of taste-stability is false in two senses: "First, social factors can affect our ordinal preferences

9. Related contributions include Lane [2000], and Diener *et alii* [2009].

– our indifference curves. But secondly, they may also affect the cardinal happiness we get from a given consumption bundle" [2006, p. 30]. Therefore, Layard argues that policy makers must account for taste formation and his approach can thus be considered a specification of the Taste Approach [2006, p. 30] [10].

Layard's reference to indifference curves indicates that preference based approaches can be employed by HE. However, insisting on the importance of happiness, preference satisfaction would for Layard's HE not be an account of well-being itself, but instead a proxy to well-being. As examples of addiction and compulsive action suggest, satisfaction of people's (unconsidered) preferences can be a poor guide to happiness. However, if policy makers possess information about satisfaction of which preferences would promote the most happiness, they can attempt to design policies that ensure that people will develop happiness promoting preferences. Thus, HE would consider the costs of preferences as low if their satisfaction leads to high W conceived as happiness.

However, Layard's points that when people's indifference curves are optimal as far as happiness is concerned, people nevertheless vary in their cardinal utility from consumption (C_R) and production (C_E). These differences cannot be captured by a purely preference based approach, and we therefore have to turn to an experienced utility measure which could indicate these happiness variations.

As shown by Sugden and Kahneman [2005], there are many ways to evaluate policies according to experienced utility. Different approaches such as question forms and brain scans have their strengths and weaknesses in terms of cost and accuracy, and scholars disagree whether they are sufficiently robust to guide policy making. A second concern with relying on experienced utility measures solely, is that the Taste Approach then would require a major methodological shift by those who practice economics today. Implementing this change might be time consuming.

10. For instance, Layard argues that "To fight the constant escalation of wants, we should prohibit commercial advertising to children, as in Sweden" [Layard 2005, p. 234].

Since many of the areas where the Taste Approach could enlighten governance (global warming, health, financial regulation etc.) seem to require new solutions urgently, this is unfortunate. A final source of concern with HE is that by its insistence on returning to Benthamite reasoning it seems to be premised on a pure mental state theory of W [Layard 2003c, p. 16-20; 2005, p. 4-5]. As shown in section 1.2, the problem with relying on Benthamite utility maximization as far as the Taste Approach is concerned is that it in principle does not provide safeguards against violation of other desiderata, and thus this specification is potentially very politically controversial.

For these three reasons, I now turn to examine two preference based specifications of the Taste Approach: LP and IPF. However, despite here not pursuing HE any further, I do not mean that this approach is necessarily unsuitable for policy making. Firstly, insofar as desire fulfillment and promotion of positive mental states both can have intrinsic value (and W effectively is a pluralistic value), HE and preference based approaches can co-exist. Furthermore, the two approaches coud be instrumentally valuable to one another. As explained above, desire fulfillment can be instrumental to happiness. Secondly, having balanced mental states might be a condition for desire fulfillment having normative force [11].

2.2. *Libertarian Paternalism and Taste Formation*

In Nudge [2008], Thaler and Sunstein argue that policy makers should use insights from Psychology and Behavioral Economics in order to improve people's decisions affecting issues such as health,

11. Discussing the conditions for paternalistic interventions, Mill writes: "[…] when there is […] only a danger of mischief, no one but the person himself can judge of the sufficiency of the motive which may prompt him to incur the risk unless he is […] delirious, or in some state of excitement or absorbation incompatible with using the full sense of the reflecting faculty, he ought, I conceive, to be only warned of the danger." [Mill 1959, p. 95]. An upshot of this view is that disrespecting a person's unconsidered desires might be legitimate when certain mental states disable a person from assessing risk soundly. By influencing people's mental states the Taste Approach could prevent these situations from emerging.

wealth and happiness. Referring to research demonstrating the impact of mechanisms as framing, anchoring and status quo biases on choices, T&S argue that preferences are context dependent entities that should not (always) be considered as exogenous variables [2008, p. 23-37]. In this manner, T&S turn away the focus from the impact of I on W to addressing the potential gain in W which improvement of choice mechanisms determining C could yield. Thus, this approach can be considered as specification of the Taste Approach.

T&S admit their proposed policy making guidelines would be in some sense paternalistic, but argue that this form of paternalism, LP, neither involves punishment, physical use of force nor economic sanctions, and that this ensures that implementation of LP would not restrict the freedom of the decision makers [2008, p. 5]: instead of giving people who are about to act irrationally a "snap" (for instance by taxation or imprisonment) LP suggests that people should be *nudged* in directions which would make their lives better: "A nudge, as we will use the term, is any aspect of the choice architecture that alters people's behavior in a predictable way without forbidding options or significantly changing economic incentives" [2008, p. 6].

T&S promise that LP is "liberty preserving" and paternalistic only in the sense that "it tries to influence choices in a way that will make choosers better off, *as judged by themselves*" [2008, p. 32, 5]. This promise, which I call the Liberty Promise, seems to render LP more politically uncontroversial than HE – at least amongst anti-paternalists.

However, it is dubious whether the Liberty Promise sits well with LP's refute of what I call the Best Interest Claim, *i.e.* "that people always (usually?) make choices that are in their best interest" [2004, p. 175]. T&S criticizes anti-paternalists in Economics for being based on this claim, which is, T&S hold, a misconception that "is either tautological, and therefore uninteresting, or testable. We claim that it is testable and false – indeed obviously false." [2004, p. 175].

Assuming that W should be determined by post-choice measures, it would be correct that the Best Interest Claim, is testable – at least in principle. An example of a post-choice measure is experienced utility expressing hedonic experiences resulting "from acts of choice" [Kahneman and Sugden 2005, p. 167]. If this sort of conception of W were compatible with the Best Interest Claim, people would always have to display perfect affective forecasting. That assumption of perfect affective forecasting is indeed testable and not self-evidently true [12].

However, experienced utility being a subgroup of mental state theories of W, it is questionable whether this and other post-choice measures are compatible with LP's Liberty Promise. For instance, we can assume that the policy makers believes that taking some drug would make Rob permanently happier. If Rob refutes taking the drug, the policy makers guided only by experienced utility measures, might might in their attempt to elevate W force Rob to take the drug [13]. Therefore, insofar as LP wants to commit to LP's Liberty Promise, policy makers can not use experienced utility measures solely.

Let us therefore consider whether the Best Interest Claim could be tested by decision utility measures such as desire fulfillment theories. Below I present two ways in which this test could be undertaken and discuss whether the W criteria that the test is based on would violate the Liberty Promise. (In the section 3 I discuss a third criterion.)

Firstly, the Best Interest Claim could be tested by asking Rob prior to his decision has been made whether the quality of his choice conditions will enable him to make future decisions in his best interest. Rob might then respond that regardless of his best

12. Recall footnote 10 on Mill's point that balanced mental states are crucial for good decision making. Consult also footnote 13 on "cooling-off periods" for arguments suggesting that a person's mental state in the first place might limit his ability to make decisions that will optimize his mental state in the second place. This point is currently echoed by those who require "cooling off policies" due to the restricting effect of excitement on rationality [Thaler and Sunstein 2008, p. 250-251].

13. Admittedly, the unwillingly happiness induced Rob might approve of the inducment after the inducment has been carried out, viz at (t+1). However, insofar as Rob disaproved of the inducement at (t−1), it is dubious whether his endorsement at (t+1) would be sufficient to render the inducement compatible with LP's Liberty Promise.

effort, he would probably make better future decisions if he were about to face better choice conditions [14]. By taking Rob's own view seriously in this way and thus presumably improving this future decisions as understood by himself subjectively, this criterion for relating to the Best Interest Claim would not have to violate the Liberty Promise if the criterion served as a guideline for policy making.

Secondly, the Best Interest Claim can be tested without testing the state of Rob at (t + 1) by examining whether the Rob at time (t) violates any basic rationality decision making principles. T&S distinguish between two systems of thinking – the Automatic System and the Reflective System [2008, p. 19]. Whereas the Reflective System is controlled, deductive and self-aware, the Automatic System is uncontrolled, associative, and unconscious. When Sunstein and Thaler suggest there should be exercised "choice architecture", it mostly concerns cases where the Automatic System otherwise would have led people to make decisions they would not have approved of, if they had been in the Reflective mode.

It is not evident that policies nudging Rob at (t + 1) in order to improve his rationality (t) would be compatible with LP's Liberty Promise. It could be argued that a libertarian conception of liberty would require that policy makers should not influence his decisions at all. By discarding Rob's decisions made by the Automatic system at (t) and making him act as he would have wanted being in his Reflective Mode at (t – 1), it seems that Rob at (t) is not considered autonomous [15]. However, provided that a consent condition is satisfied, it is not evident that nudging Rob at (t) would violate (a libertarian understanding of) the Liberty Promise. Provided that the policy maker knows that Rob at (t – 1) prefers acting rationally

14. Footnote between 10, 11 and 12 give examples of favorable and non-favorable choice conditions due to (in this sense) unfortunate mental states.

15. Thus, LP's distinction between the two systems of thinking echoes Berlin's distinction between higher and lower self which according to Berlin is important for those who endorse a positive conception of liberty [1969].

as a result of a nudge at (t) to acting irrationally and not being nudged, the Liberty Promise would arguably not be violated[16].

The challenges for LP then, is firstly to efficiently identify the cases where this condition empirically holds and secondly to determine whether it is any cases ethically permissible for the policy makers to ignore this consent restriction. If it is permissible, then the view that a nudge and rationality is being preferred to irrationality and no nudge, could legitimately be used as an assumption in areas of governance where this condition usually holds, and thus function as measure of testing the Best Interest Claim.

3. BEYOND LIBERTARIAN PATERNALISM

Here, I examine a third specification of the Taste Approach: Inexpensive Preference Formation (IPF). Being a preference based theory, this specification can be considered a guideline for governance that extends and transcends LP.

3.1. *Inexpensive Preference Formation*

A third decision utility based criterion for testing the Best Interest Claim not addressed in 2.2 is based on the following premise: it is an upshot of desire fulfillment theories that W can be increased by developing "different basic desires that are easier to satisfy" [Arneson 2006, p. 12]. Based on this premise the Best

16. The merits of the Automatic system as a generator of good decisions should not be underestimated. Firstly, as the Automatic system is unconscious and automatic, it could be that its employment requires less energy than the Reflective System. Secondly, by making decisions by the Automatic System and not only by the Reflective System, Rob diversifies risk – insofar as deductive inferences made by the Reflective System are vulnerable of being systematically wrong in the case the premises from which conclusions are deduced are false. Thirdly, the Automatic system being associative, it is a source of inductively acquired information, firstly based on previous positive and negative experiences of Rob, and secondly, through evolutionary history of his ancestors. Note, however, that this does have to mean that this system as a generator of decisions is not improvable by LP's nudges or other specifications of the Taste Approach. Rob fearing water due to inductively acquired associations from traumatic childhood experiences when he could not swim, should perhaps be reduced when he later has learned to swim.

Interest Claim can be tested by examining whether people make decisions based on desires that are as easy to satisfy as they possibly could have been.

The following example shows the logic behind this reasoning. Let us consider Dave's preferences for two goods: silver (S) and gold (G). Assume that (S) is less expensive than (G), and that Dave has a limited budget for these goods. Suppose that Dave at time (t) considers G as desirable and is neutral about S. By (t+1) his preferences have changed and he is now neutral about G and desires S. I indicating his income and P_G and P_S indicating the prices of G and S respectively, his demand functions (d_1) and (d_2) at (t) and (t+1) would then be as follows [Varian 1999, p. 81]:

(d_1): $G = I/P_G$
(d_2): $S = I/P_S$

Since $P_G > P_S$, Dave gets more of his desired consumption bundles at (t+1) than at (t), His indifference curves (indicated by the horizontal and vertical lines) and budget constraints (indicated by the diagonal lines) at (t) and (t+1) are indicated by Figure 2 and 3. Premised on basic decision theory principles, Dave's optimal choices in both instances have boundary optimums indicated by G* and S* in figure 1 and 2 respectively [Varian 1999, p. 76]. As S* is further away from *origin* than G*, the new preferences makes Dave better off at (t+1) than (t) [17].

The increase in W has been caused not by a change of his budget line, but of his indifference curves. Thus, a standard for comparison of sets of preferences accounting for other factors than completeness, transitivity and reflexivity is identified. W increasing without I having increased, it follows from (r*) that C effectively is lower at t_2 than at t_1. The higher the potential gain in W is by adjusting preferences, the higher is C. Governance reducing C as here specified, increases W. Thus, a third specification of

17. Being premised on basic principles of decision theory this conclusion requires that Dave at both (t) and (t+1) has the capacity to choose optimally given his preferences and income and the prices for the two goods. In the case Dave at these moments does not possess these capacities, rationality enhancing nudges of LP can accompany what I below call IPF.

the Taste Approach is identified: The doctrine of Inexpensive Preference Formation (IPF).

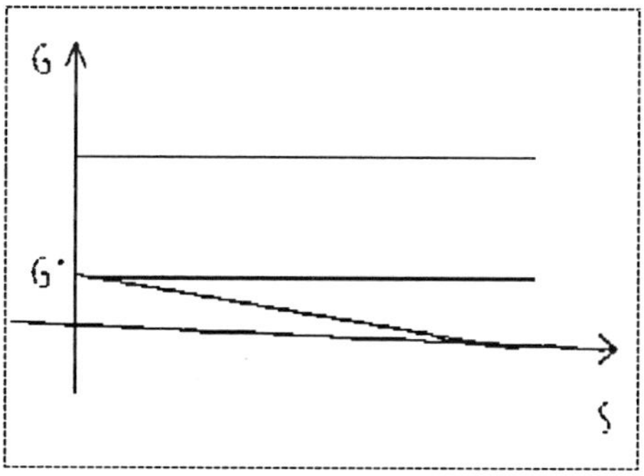

Figure 2: (t)

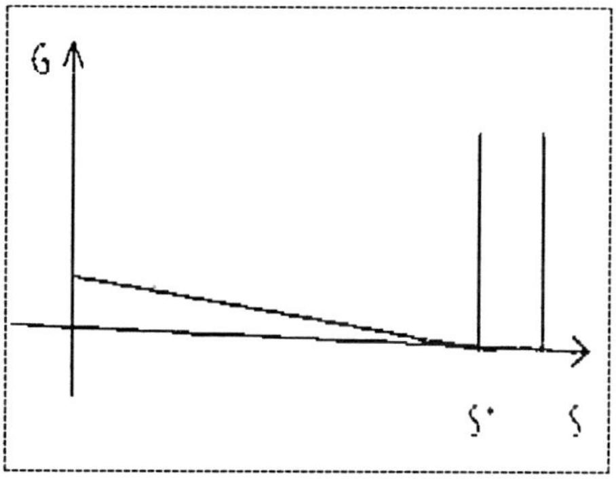

Figure 3: (t + 1)

According to IPF, policies should initiate choice architecture in cases when there is no "irrationality" as understood by LP. Dave making deductive decisions in his Reflective Mode at t_1, must necessarily deduce choices from premises (desires) indicating the ends he wants to reach. Despite Dave's reflective mode at (t) it is not unlikely that these desires at (t − 1) have been influenced through context sensitive desire formation processes [Bornstein 1968; Zajonc 1968]. Based on the above definition of C, the Best Interest Claim can be tested by investigating whether the shape and slopes of Dave's indifference curves at t could have been shaped in a more optimal way at (t − 1).

3.2. *Two restrictions and their modifications*

The need for restrictive measures limiting the extent to which policy makers should develop inexpensive preferences amongst the citizens can be illustrated by the anecdote of the horseman who got depressed because his best horse had died – the one that he had schooled into not eating and who was now just about learning not to consume water. In order to help policy makers not to repeat these sort of mistakes, I here present two restrictions designed to prevent IPF from not being used unwisely: The Consent Requirement and the Pluralistic Well-being-Restriction.

Let us first examine whether IPF could be compatible with the Liberty Promise described in 2.2. Based on the arguments used in discussing the compatibility between rationality improving nudges and the Liberty Promise, it follows that IPF would only be consistent with the Liberty Promise if Dave's preference changes (provided that they are institutionally induced) from (t) to (t + 1) were authorized by Dave himself at (t– 1). This is a strict restriction of IPF and I do not here assume that this "Consent Requirement" *always* should block IPF. By the end of this section I propose that policy makers in certain circumstances face a trade-off between concerns to consent and libertarian liberty on the one hand and the gain achieved by reducing C on the other hand [18].

A further complication concerning trade-offs between liberty and W is that the sensible policy maker should (as the anecdote taught us) not merely consider the impact of preference changes on the immediate gain in Dave's W understood as desire fulfillment, but also account for both short and long term effects, not only on future desire fulfillment, but also on W as determined by other sensible accounts. As suggested in 2.2 there is a possibility that W is a pluralistic notion which assigns intrinsic value both to

18. A problem with the Consent Requirement presented above is that can be practically challenging to control when there is consent for preference changes. I will here follow the discussion of this problem in 2.2 and suggest that policy makers could examine areas of governance where this condition *usually* holds. This proposal clearly being problematic from libertarian perspective, and I here provide no knock down argument that the libertarian worry is not groundless.

desire fulfillment, positive mental states and the development of one's capabilities. Given that the relevant literature on W lacks indisputable arguments showing that only one of its theories is reasonable, it is a sound principle of governance to diversify risk and not put all the eggs in the same basket. Based on this pragmatic approach, I propose that policy makers should initiate IPF when the less resource demanding sets of preferences is approved of by other plausible accounts of W. Examples of such preferences could be preferences for engaging in productive and health promoting activities. Let me call this restriction the Pluralistic Well-being Restriction.

Having presented two restrictions, let me consider two ways in which these restrictions could be modified. Firstly, I suggest that the Consent Requirement should not block IPF policies, such as for instance provision of information about the benefit of simple living, provided the following requirement is not violated: Dave must be aware of what is going on and the information must be provided in a way that ensures that Dave has the opportunity to reflect about whether he should include the value of for instance simple living in his value system and autonomously form (first order) preferences for instance for jewelry or means of transport according to that value[19]. This modification of the Consent Requirement I call the Process Modification.

Those who would reject that Dave has the necessary cognitive capacities that this reflection process would require, have reasons to be correspondingly concerned about whether Dave has the necessary capacities to handle information from business advertisement and market players. Since commercial companies have no immediate economic incentive to provide information for goods for which they cannot charge, citizens of market economies will be exposed to information about commercial goods to a disproportionate extent. Thus, there seems to be an information-failure in the market for goods and activities that are *gratis*, like walking in

19. As argued by Mill, concerns to person's best interests "are good reasons for remonstrating with him, or reasoning with him, or persuading him but not for compelling him or visiting him with any evil" [1859, p. 9].

public parks or engaging in voluntary work [20]. This market failure can be corrected for in two ways. Either by banning advertisement altogether, or by providing information for public and other *gratis* goods. From the perspective of businesses it would be expected that the second solution would be perceived as the one which violates their liberties the least.

A potentially important gain in this context by correcting for this information failure at (t−2), would be that the consequently better informed Dave would be likely to make better judgments when policy makers guided by the Consent Requirement asks him at (t−1) whether he in order to reduce C at (t) prefers being nudged by means that he cannot autonomously control.

Whereas the Process Modification only modified the Consent Requirement and not the Pluralistic Well-being Restrictions, I now present a second modification which applies to both these restrictions of IPF. Recall from 1.1 that an essential factor in determining the conditions for Taste Approach policies being legitimate, hinges on whether arguments against Taste Approach policies should be considered as side constraints or as concerns that can be traded off against the gain that Taste Approach policies could yield. An interesting intermediate condition worth further investigation holds that the Consent Requirement and the Pluralistic Well-being Restriction are not as absolute side constraints, but instead conditional constraints that under particularly pressing circumstances would lose their status as side constraints and turn into concerns that should be traded against the gain that IPF and other Taste Approach policies could yield.

Provided that this is a sensible line of reasoning, it is a matter of judgment whether the current global situation with enormous inequalities, danger of global warming and mental and physical health problems should count as circumstances where the two restrictions should lose their status as side constraints. According to the recently launched Worldwatch Institute report "2010 State of the World – Transforming Cultures from Consumerism to

20. For further discussion of this information-failure see Otterholt [2005, p. 45-46].

Sustainability" our global circumstances in the current decade indeed seem to require measures that appear to correspond with extensive use of the Taste Approach. As it is argued under the subtitle "Cultivating Cultures of Sustainability" in the report chapter "The Rise and Fall of Consumer Cultures": "Yes, altering a system's rules (with legislation, for instance) can change a system too, but not fundamentally. These will typically produce only incremental changes. Today more systematic change is needed." [Erik Assadourian 2010, p. 16]

CONCLUSION

In this article I have examined three specifications of the Taste Approach: HE, LP and IPF. Proposing a pragmatic approach to theories of W understood as a pluralistic notion, both HE, LP and IPF can be useful constituents in Taste Approach policy making. Whereas all the three specifications have their virtues, they must at the same time be used judicially in the perspective of other normative concerns. HE should not neglect the value of autonomy, LP should relate critically to the assumption that everyone prefer to be nudged in order remove irrationalities, and IPF should be balanced against the "Consent Requirement" and the "Pluralistic Well-being Condition".

In order to make decisions as efficiently as required by current circumstances of governance, HE, LP and IPF must be guided by clear methodological approaches. Of these three candidates as far as they currently are developed, LP gets the highest score on this particular aspect since all it lacks in order to be employed efficiently is a way to test the assumption that people would prefer a nudge in order to act rationality. Challenges for HE in this respect is firstly associated worries concerned with experienced utility measures, and secondly with the lack of (clear) normative self-restricting criteria for the promotion of happiness. Whilst IPF, on the other hand has two self-restricting criteria, the Consent Requirement and the Pluralistic Well-being Restriction, I have thus far not provided clear procedures for how the policy makers should obtain the knowledge required by these restrictions.

In addition to these concerns, the Taste Approach faces several practical and normative challenges concerning models of governance with which various specifications of the Taste Approach could be compatible. Consider the following three models of governance that could affect taste formation:

(1) Direct central governance exercised by governmental bodies at international, national and local level.
(2) Indirect central governance through the strengthening of civil societies and private public partnership.
(3) Indirect central governance through the facilitation of market institutions.

For the central governance skeptic the third model might be attractive. The question then, would be whether there exist markets facilitating optimization of C. Examples from the current market suggesting that there is a market for taste changes are the business of self-help books, couching and perhaps also part of the cultural industry such as theatre and weekly magazines. By turning to suppliers who (according to the judgments of the consumers) would have positive impact on their taste formation, Dave himself would have a chance to influence his future taste formation. The extent to which this market succeeds should be accounted for by the policy maker who considers whether inexpensive tastes should be cultivated. Potential challenges with the market solution include the worry that those who most urgently need to adjust their tastes might not benefit from the market solution – firstly they might not afford it; or secondly, because failure of consumer sovereignty might not enable them to fully utilize these markets.

Not having investigated these empirical matters in this article, I give here no finite answers to the questions that they raise, but instead conclude that given the attractive features of the Taste Approach, these questions are worth further pursuit. Given the potential gain that Taste Approach policies might yield, reasons for *not* consulting the Taste Approach when policies are designed ought to be good if they are prevail. As argued by Mill: "Human beings owe to each other help to distinguish the better from the worse and encouragement to choose the former and avoid the latter." [1859, p. 74].

REFERENCES

ASSADOURIAN E., 2010, "The Rise and Fall of Consumerist Cultures", in *2010 State of the World – Transforming Cultures – From Consumerism to Sustainability – A Wordlwatch Inistitute Report on Progress Toward a Sustainable Society.*

BERLIN I., 1969, *Four Essays on Liberty*, Oxford, Oxford University Press.

COHEN G.A., 1989, "On the Currency of Egalitarian Justice", *Ethics*, vol. 99, p. 906-944.

– 2004, "Expensive Taste Rides Again", *in* J. Burley (ed.), *Dworkin and his Critics*, Oxford, Blackwell.

DIENER E. *et alii*, *Well-being for Public Policy*, Oxford, Oxford University Press.

DWORKIN R., 2000, *Sovereign Virtue*, Cambridge (Mass.), Harvard University Press.

EASTERLIN R.A., 1974, "Does Economic Growth Improve the Human Lot?", *in* P. David and M. Reder (eds.), *Nations and Households in Economic Growth: Essays in Honor of Moses Abramovitz*, New York, Academic Press Inc.

FRANKFURT H., 1988, *The Importance of What We Care About*, Cambridge, Cambridge University Press.

FREY B. *et alii*, 2002, *Happiness and Economics*, Princeton, University Press.

Griffin J., 1986, *Well-Being*, Oxford, Clarendon Press.

HELLEVIK O., 2008, *Jakten på den norske lykken*, Oslo, Universitetsforlaget.

KAHNEMAN D. and SUGDEN R., 2005, "Experienced utility as a standard of policy evaluation", *Environmental and Resource Economics*, 32, p. 161-181.

LANE R., 2000, *The Loss of Happiness in Market Economies*, New Haven, YUP.

LAYARD R., 2003, "Happiness: Has Social Science a Clue?", *Lionel Robins Memorial Lectures 2002/3.*

– 2005, *Happiness – Lessons From A New Science*, London, Penguin Group.

MILL J.S., 1859 (1978), *On Liberty*, Cambridge, Hackett Publishing.

NOZICK R., 1974, *Anarchy, State, and Utopia*, Oxford, Blackwell.

OLSON M., 1971, *The Logic of Collective Action*, Cambridge (Mass.), Harvard University Press.

OSWALD, 1997, "Happiness and Economic Performance", *Economic Journal*, 107, p. 1815-1831.

OTTERHOLT T., 2005, *Should the State Cultivate Cheaper Tastes?*, M. Phil. Thesis, Oxford, online at http://folk.uio.no/torotte/Should_the_State_Cultivate_Cheaper_Tastes_Otterholt2005.doc

PARFIT D., 1984, *Reasons and Persons*, Oxford, Clarendon Press.

ROZATI C.S., 2006, "Preference-Formation and the Personal Good", *in* S. Olsaretti, *Preferences and Well-being*, Cambridge, Cambridge University Press.

STEVENSON B. and WOLFERS S.B., 2008, "Economic Growth and Happiness: Reassessing the Easterlin Paradox", *Brookings Papers on Economic Activity*, Spring 2008, p. 1-87.

THALER R.H. and SUNSTEIN C.R., "Libertarian Paternalism", *Economic American Review*, vol. 93, n° 2, p. 175-179.

– 2008, *Nudge*, New Haven, YUP.

VARIAN H., 1999, *Intermediate Economics – A Modern Approach*, New York, Norton Inc.

From gross misconduct to responsible behaviour a dream that necessitates realisticness

Vinca Bigo*

Résumé

Les discours sur le développement durable auront peu de substance, tant qu'ils ne seront pas accompagnés d'une notion de responsabilité, qui elle est reliée à la durabilité, où encore à la soutenabilité. *Cet article est motivé par des circonstances tant géopolitiques qu'économiques calamiteuses, en terme de gouvernance, et de manière plus générale, par la prolifération de pratiques que l'on qualifiera ni de soutenables, ni de responsables.* En *conséquence, j'ai pour but l'élaboration d'une conception de la responsabilité, elle ancrée et robuste. Dans ce projet, je m'efforcerai d'identifier tout particulièrement les conditions nécessaires pour un tendre vers un comportement responsable, capable de soutenir un développement dit durable en pratique, aussi bien qu'en théorie.*

Mots clés : *responsabilité, réalisme moral, psychologie morale, distorsion, genre*

Abstract

There is little substance in discourses of sustainable development, unless they are sustained by a credible notion of responsibility. My paper is motivated by a dire state of affairs, the ubiquitous failure of governance, and, more generally, the proliferation of widespread non sustainable and irresponsible practices. Consequently, my project is to develop a grounded understanding of

* V. Bigo: Associate Professor in Gender, Ethics and Leadership at Euromed Management, Marseille (France), vinca.bigo@euromed-management.com and occasional lecturer at Cambridge University, vb243@cam.ac.uk.

responsibility, and to seek out the particular conditions necessary for responsible conduct, one liable to underpin socially sustainable development in practice.

Keywords: responsibility, moral realism, moral psychology, distortion, gender

JEL Classification: Q56 (Sustainability), A13 (Relation of Economics to Social Values), P16 (Political Economy)

INTRODUCTION [1]

In 1987, the Brundtland Report did much to popularise the notion of sustainable development. The report offers us the following definition: "development that meets the needs of the present without compromising the ability of future generations to meet their own needs" [2]. Two decades on, the literature on the subject is prolific. Sustainability is often considered to necessitate that we take into consideration three spheres: environmental, social and economic, an approach also known as the *triple bottom line*. The importance given to each sphere typically varies with the interested parties or stakeholders.

There is an aspect of sustainability, however, that has received comparatively little attention, but on which sustainable development crucially depends. And this is the question of responsibility. Responsibility is of course a key tenant of governance. For development to be sustainable it needs to be conceived and conducted in a responsible manner. Recent events in global markets indicate, in no uncertain terms, the potentially dire consequences of inappropriate governance.

The objective of this paper is to flesh out the notion of responsibility, an under theorised aspect of governance and sustainability. To conceptualise responsibility in a global economy, in the context of markets, and human aspirations to well being and

1. I wish to thank both Miriam Teschl and Tony Lawson for bringing helpful and constructive comments to earlier versions of this paper, as well as the organisers and attendants of the Cambridge based workshop out of which this paper emerged.

2. http://www.ace.mmu.ac.uk/eae/Sustainability/Older/Brundtland_Report.html

flourishing, I must draw on economic, philosophical, psycho-analytical, and gendered analytical theory and perspectives. Specifically, when turning to psychology, I shall consider certain aspects of child development that bear on responsibility.

I shall argue that a responsible, and so sustainable development, involves both a particular orientation of care or concern, and a related human capability [3] to produce caring outcomes. As such, responsibility is not a strictly deontological concept, according to which a set of categorical rules or imperatives are somehow willed onto individuals. The duty presupposes that there is an *ability to respond*, an ability that I take to correspond to a human disposition that we individuals need to actively develop in our relations with others (and the world more generally).

In writing this paper, I am in large part motivated by the growing misconduct we are witnessing on a global scale, with very often devastating consequences, a conduct that by all means warrants the label of irresponsible behaviour. Whilst for centuries plenty has been said and written about *what* one should or should not do, there has been comparatively very little concern with *how* individuals actually develop and/or acquire the ability to behave as responsible citizens. Consequently, the objective of this paper is to produce a notion of responsibility as *dynamic or processual*, one that goes beyond mere moral imperative. It is to develop a more operational notion of responsibility, and to unpack some of the obstacles and possible leverages to becoming a responsible individual, capable of adopting responsible behaviour.

3. I am aware that the term *capability* is employed in specific ways by Amartya Sen and Martha Nussbaum [Sen 1982; Nussbaum 1995]. Whilst I do engage with these authors elsewhere in my work, the meaning of 'capability' here is not restricted to the one intended by Sen. Indeed, following an article by Sabina Alkire [2005], one in which she sets out to clarify some of Sen's central concepts, it transpires that "capabilities are various combinations of functionings (beings and doings) that the person can achieve… Put differently, they are 'the substantive freedoms he or she enjoys to lead the kind of life he or she has reason to value'" [Alkire 2005, p. 2]. Responsibility, as intended in this paper, encompasses both functionings and capabilities. Thus, when employing the term capability, capacity, skill, and ability, I do so in a wider sense than found in the capabilities approach.

To do so, and to dissipate likely confusion, involves me, first, drawing out the distinction between ethics and morality. For responsibility is variously associated with both spheres. I then discuss, in the third section of this paper, the possibility of being a realist rather than a relativist about ethics and morality. I must do so because the notion of responsibility I advance is entirely bound up with realism, and the possibility thereof. In section four, I discuss determinism and free will, and the limits of these philosophies that frequently underpin ethics and morality.

These preliminary sections clear the ground and set the scene for me to introduce responsibility as dynamic and processual, articulated along (three) different axes. Here, will I also introduce the different conditions necessary for meeting responsibilities. Yet a further section examines one of these conditions in particular: the capacity or ability to respond. I next devote a section to a discussion of two approaches to ethics and morality that share features with my own. Finally, I explore some of the concrete or practical implications of my analysis for shaping (more) responsible individuals. Here, I suggest moving away from gender stereotypical identities, given the existence of certain gender related *ethically* responsible orientations and *moral* ability to successfully meet our responsibilities, before making my concluding comments.

ETHICS AND MORALITY

Before examining the notion of responsibility more closely, I must first of all, if briefly, examine the distinction between ethics and morality. This seems to be a quasi necessary step to arrive at a clear understanding of responsibility, for responsibility involves a form of both ethics and morality. In essence, *morality is concerned with actual moral conduct. We can define morality as the domain of applied ethics.* In others words, ethics is guiding of morality. On this count, we can distinguish between a framework of *ethical* principles, on the one hand, including our ethical orientation or virtues. And we find, often complex, concrete situations in which *moral* actions take place, on the other.

The ethical is merely taken as *what applies throughout* (transfactually[4]), posited irrespective of particular actions. Indeed, typically, to facilitate flourishing, if that is the goal, it is preferable for most of us to respect a number of pre established ethical rules. Following a Kantian perspective, morally good behaviour prescribes that we stick to specified ethical rules no matter the context. At the other extreme, it may be thought that the most appropriate way of behaving requires us to apply a different *a priori* established rule or ethical position. The latter being that one should take decisions about moral action once, and only once, we have assessed the specific relational context, so as to minimise harm and maximise well being. In order words, the *a priori* rule in such cases is to establish *a posteriori* what behaviour is best adopted.

We can in practice, of course, not ignore context. This is so, if only because context contributes to both facilitate and constrain our actions. Indeed, as noted above, when leaving the realm of ethical abstraction, we necessarily deal with circumstances, in which ethical norms and values are *applied*, at which point we enter the realm of morality. Typically, contexts complexify matters considerably. The imperatives "do not lie", or "do not kill", are examples of ethical positions or propositions. Whilst in the abstract lying is almost universally considered to be (and in all likelihood is too) wrong, under certain circumstances, it will be found that lying may save innocent lives. So in practice, moral actors can in the end be seen to strike a balance between (partly out of circumstantial necessity) various ethical propositions to adapt to specific circumstances.

So how do we differentiate between responsibility as 1) ethics and 2) morality? Remember, morality is ethics in practice, or applied ethics. When referring to responsibility as a moral obligation, moral philosophers have variously intended responsibility as 1) a principle, an *a priori* responsibility towards others human beings, oneself, animals, plants, etc., 2) a virtuous orientation, and

4. Something operating transfactually refers to a force or tendency that is in play, where actual and/or observable outcomes will often be the result of a combination of transfactual tendencies [Lawson 1997].

3) the specific moral conduct through which persons will be held accountable and judged. As indicated above, for the purposes of my paper, I intend and use morality, in the latter sense (or scenario). That is, I take morality as applicable to conduct. Ethics, on the other hand, I intend to include both 1) principles and 2) a virtuous orientation.

Let me offer two short examples, by way of illustration. A conscientious objector can be considered as failing to meet her responsibility as a citizen, where military service is in force. As such, her conduct is *morally* irresponsible. At the same time, on some conceptions of the good society, her orientation is defendable, in which case it is *ethically* responsible. Conversely, a concentration camp guard fulfils her responsibility in watching over and likely mal treating prisoners, whilst simultaneously clearly failing to follow certain ethical principles.

In this section, I presented the distinction between ethical principles and orientation, on the one hand, and moral conduct on the other[5], with the corollaries of responsibility from an ethical and from a moral perspective, respectively. Below, I clarify what I mean by moral and ethical realism, thus further clearing the ground for my analysis of responsibility.

CAN WE BE REALISTS ABOUT ETHICS AND MORALITY?

Moral (and ethical) realism is a philosophical tradition, according to which there is 1) a reality to the world, including the world of non visible things, such as thoughts and ideas, independently or our knowing about it, where 2) a thing, object, action, thought, and so on, is real in virtue of its having an effect, 3) we may be right or wrong about things[6], 4) including about ethical

5. I am aware that it is possible to conceive of orientation as a form of behaviour or conduct, and so morality. For the purposes of the paper, however, I have allocated orientation as pertaining to the realm of principles, and so ethics.

6. The tendency to reduce our understanding of the world to what is "directly" observable, and to refer to the latter as factual, is one best known and described as *naïve*

propositions and moral actions, and 5) that that which is ethically true and morally good at any point in time depends on the way the world is (irrespective of our perception of it). I should add that such a stance does not in any way suggest that our perceptions do not have an effect on the way the world reproduces and transforms itself, a world that is dynamic, or always in process [Lawson 1997].

The moral realist tradition, with which philosopher ranging from Aristotle (384-323 BCE) to American philosophers George E. Moore [1903] have been associated, demarcates itself most notedly perhaps from moral (and ethical) relativism. According the latter, that which is moral and/or ethical depends on our perceptions (or interpretations). Whilst a moral (and ethical) realist would argue that perceptions certainly make a difference, a relativistic position suggests that perceptions are *all* there is to the matter, and that there can, consequently, be no reality to ethics and morality (and to the world more generally), and so, it further contends, no truth to the matter either [for a realist position in economics, see Lawson 2000].

I have indicated that the object of morality is with actual moral behaviour or actions, and that ethics acts as a guide to morality. Morality is connected to our practices that take place in specific contexts that typically involve many factors that lie outside of our control. Relatedly, evaluating the consequences of our actions is often difficult, whether in respect of what is taking place here and now, or of what lies beyond.

Both ethical standards and moral behaviour are subject to continuing discussion and disagreement. Especially in the domain of applied ethics, that is, morality, we are constantly confronted with cultural and context specific differences in evaluation and judgment. Perceptions and interpretations are never neutral, objective, or impartial. Individuals follow and judge moral actions through personally and collectively constructed lenses. Different cultures and traditions have over time produced different moral

realism. This approach tends to downplay the fact that "facts" are necessarily mediated by our lenses, our perception of things.

codes of conduct. Such codes are implicitly and/or explicitly backed by the community, following written and/or tacit collective agreements. Their violation will often lead to some form of sanction. The latter may include shaming, financial penalties, bodily sanctions, and so on.

The Global North, for instance, has a tendency to consider that nature should be controlled and exploited for the benefit of humanity. Indeed, nature has increasingly been instrumentalised, especially since the western world began making natural scientific discoveries that challenged religious dogma. The new found knowledge inspired both scientists and philosophers to try and discipline nature, a process described by Susan Bordo in a book entitled *The Flight to Objectivity: Essays on Cartesianism and Culture*:

> As in much of early modern science and philosophy – in Bacon, most dramatically – the dream of knowledge is here imagined as an explicit revenge fantasy, an attempt to wrest back control from nature. [Bordo 1987, p. 75]

On the other hand, the Global South often associates nature with the Divine. A respect for nature is then considered important, along side human flourishing, though in practice global capitalism increasingly dictates otherwise [Shiva 1989]. Other sources of difference in evaluating moral conduct stem from the sometimes very particular and personal ways in which individuals experience (possibly) shared events [7].

Moral decisions thus tend to be complicated to make, and moral behaviour equally often difficult to judge (as good or bad). Difficulty of evaluation should not, however, be confused with there being no reality, and so no truth to the matter either. Our observation of differences in ethical and moral standards does not signify that we cannot at the same be realists about both ethics and morality. By this, I mean that our orientations and actions can be deemed ethical and moral, or not as the case may be, *independently of our knowing about it.*

7. Note that siblings, even when raised by the same parents, often experience and recall events very differently [Apter 2008].

To take an example, a child who wishes to watch TV all day or eat lots of ice cream, at some level certainly is convinced that this will contribute to her well being. Yet, it is unlikely that these indulgences truly benefit the child. Two considerations ensue. First, whether the child, the community, and so on, *agree* on, and accurately *appraise*, what principles are ethically right and wrong, and whether the behaviour is morally good or bad. Second, the *truth* of the matter irrespective of appraisal and agreement.

Now, the subject of appraisal has inspired much of the more recent literature on responsibility, one sparked by Peter Strawson's seminal text *Freedom and Resentment* [1962]. The central question is whether we can accurately, or "objectively", attribute responsibility to a moral agent, and her actions. The focus of the discussion is on the theorist/observer's capacity to accurately *evaluate*.

This, I recognise, is a crucial question. But evaluation seemingly concerns all forms of abstraction of thought, and not just theories of responsibility. It may thus be sufficient to note, in line with a (moral) realist conception of the world, that we are *fallible* in our judgements, appraisals, evaluations, in so far as we can be wrong about the object of our abstractions, thoughts, theories. I am in truth not convinced the ability to accurately *apportion* responsibility warrants featuring so centrally in debates on responsibility. Possibly, one might more usefully concern oneself with the process of its actual exercise, and less with the attribution of blame or praise.

In sum, on a moral realist conception, propositions can be either ethically *right or wrong*, and moral actions either *good or bad*. This is so even 1) whilst ethical and moral frameworks can be seen to vary across cultures and individuals, so that disagreement exists over what is right and wrong, good or bad, and 2) when there is possibly ultimately no way of verifying with certainty which assessment is correct, and which is false[8]. Disagreements on what is best for humanity, and as to what constitutes flourishing, especially

8. We can nonetheless get a fairly good idea of whether assertions hold, if only by verifying they are not internally contradictory, at one level, and by their proving robust in the face of real life event, that is, in concrete situations, on the other.

when we move away from more abstract notions of flourishing, are ubiquitous. As such, assessments may be very difficult to make, but whether ethically or morally, there is a truth of the matter. Agreement has little to do with it, for truth is not a matter of a majority being convinced of a particular matter[9]. Before coming to a full definition of responsibility, I must in the next section briefly discuss the question of free will in ethical and moral context.

Between free will and determinism

The question of free will is a (further) facet of responsibility that has been centrally considered in theories of responsibility, perhaps from the very onset of discussions on the subject. Aristotle argued that a condition for being able to attribute (moral) responsibility, and so praise or blame someone, was that people should be able to act freely. This debate then centres on whether one adopts a form of (strong) causal determinism[10], or if to the contrary one believes people have (absolute or relative) freedom of choice in their actions. For, it makes sense to apportion blame or praise, only on the latter conception of human behaviour.

Thus, free will is a condition for the attribution of blame or praise. Certainly, I do assume, in my conception of human behaviour, that, often, or at least under certain circumstances, persons had the possibility to act otherwise than they did. Once more, though the question of free will is a condition for being able to attribute responsibility at all, it leaves unexamined some key aspects of responsibility (which I develop below). But there is, first

9. This is not to take away the merits of democracy, in particular, of processes of participative democracy. Indeed, such processes of exchange may be most helpful in being able to accurately answer ethical and moral questions.

10. Determinism as a philosophical position takes on various forms. It comes in degrees of "hardness", veering towards fatalism, and of "softness". It typically considers there to be limitations in, or absence of, freedom of choice. This it believes is caused by higher organising principles, scientific, or theological, that limit or take away our freedom of action. The latter position was centrally explored by Augustine (354-430) and Aquinas (1225-1274).

of all, a further aspect to *(free) will*, and this is the question of *will power*, that I must address here.

Over the centuries, moral character and integrity have been centrally discussed in moral/ethical scholarship. Indeed, human behaviour is at least in part contingent on the character of the moral actor. For a long time scholars conceived will to be a dominant factor in moral behaviour. They argued individuals needed, by an act of will, to master the darker side of their character, their inner monsters and demons. Specifically, *rational reasoning* and introspection, and control of mind over body (and separate from matter) have been commonly advanced as vectors for developing one's moral character. These approaches to ethics and morality can be traced back to ancient Greek philosophers, and later to the influential Saint Augustine (354-430), currents that have inspired much of western philosophy to this day [11].

Though by some recognised to be emotionally complex, the tendency in moral philosophy and theosophy has been to think of moral agents, including specifically responsible agents, through 1) a rather black box notion of "rationality" and *will power* to conquer one's weaknesses, whilst 2) down playing restrictions on person's freedom of action and thought. Constraints may result from (internal) factors, such as contradictory feelings, or falsely held beliefs, and/or from (external) factors, such as the complex webs of human relations, or collective obligations. Moral behaviour is, as indicated, tied to human practice. It is questionable therefore that mere will power and reason constitute sufficient and satisfactory criterion to produce responsible outcomes.

With the onset of Marxism, as well as with contemporary psychoanalysis and deconstructivist trends (including social constructivism and post modernism), persons came to be understood in terms of their personal life histories, their upbringing, and not least their (intelligible but) unconscious motives for actions.

11. These approaches to responsibility are the work of essentially male philosophers and research communities. Arguably, systematic female scholarly production may have yielded alternative notions of ethics, morality, and responsibility, a point to which I shall return in due course.

Yet, certainly post structuralist and deconstructivist approaches, have produced limitations of their own. According to these schools, the individual is determined by language systems (a linguistic form of determinism), in which free will ends up escaping her. She is subject to processes to which she can but surrender. There is no individual or subjectivity left to speak of.

In truth, neither mere reason, and decontextualised free will (or unconstrained freedom of choice), nor determinism, constitute adequate paradigms to frame moral behaviour. Both some degree of awareness and free will are necessarily assumed, if we are to impute responsibility on actors at all. But it makes little sense to cast a person as perfectly free and unconstrained, internally (psychically) and externally, in her actions. In reality, external circumstances, and a person's particular internal dispositions, will in part enable, and in part constrain, her choices. Having clarified a number of central issues that frame the question of responsibility, we can now turn to its definition.

Responsibility as process

The Miriam Webster online dictionary[12] offers various meanings for the concept of responsibility:

> 1.*a*: liable to be called on to answer *b* (*1*): liable to be called to account as the primary cause, motive, or agent <a committee responsible for the job> (*2*): being the cause or explanation <mechanical defects were responsible for the accident> *c*: liable to legal review or in case of fault to penalties
> 2.*a*: able to answer for one's conduct and obligations: trustworthy b: able to choose for oneself between right and wrong
> 3: marked by or involving responsibility or accountability <responsible financial policies> <a responsible job>
> 4: politically answerable; *especially*: required to submit to the electorate if defeated by the legislature – usedespecially of the British cabinet

12. http://www.merriam-webster.com/dictionary/responsible.

Below, I advance a notion of responsibility[13] as *process* like. On such a conception, responsibility is in the first instance, and as often conceptualised, a duty or obligation to follow a particular course of action[14].

Responsibility can be, and often is, thought of as the obligation to act in coherence with a particular ethical framework of reference. If very often this framework is left implicit, one necessarily underpins the creation and attribution of responsibility, and so obligations. Behaving responsibly, then, consists first in fulfilling one's obligation, whatever its nature. What kind of duty is contained in any particular obligation will further depend on the ethical framework of reference.

The production of a responsible outcome in moral terms entails at the minimum the fulfilment of one's obligations. An additional requirement, for responsibility to emerge in ethical terms, is the correct identification of such obligations. It is quite possible, and it often seems the case these days, that objectives, such as seeking growth at all cost, are not responsible, in the sense of not being especially conducive to the flourishing of all, and so not compatible with coherent ethical principles. This may be so even if moral agents scrupulously carry out their given responsibility.

Responsible outcomes and accurately meeting the stated duty contained in this or that responsibility are thus not the same. Put differently, it may be the case that both the ethical framework of reference, and obligations contained in the responsibilities (attributed) are accurately apprehended, so as to successfully overcome, for example, this or that crisis. Note that even such a configuration is not entirely sufficient to guarantee a responsible outcome. For it may be that agents subsequently fail to carry their obligations (correctly), and as such do not act responsibly.

13. Note in passing that in discussing responsibility, the term is variously declined as noun, responsibility, adverb, responsibly, and as adjective, responsible.

14. To be responsible also simply means "to be the cause of", or *a posteriori* to be held as responsible, but this is not typically how I (or most) intend it in the context of moral and/or ethical discussions.

Now, when it is one's responsibility to do x or y, one is also held accountable, by one self and/or others, for carrying out the given obligation. *Sanctions* of some sort are further applied upon failure to perform one's duty. Indeed, the notion of responsibility and so obligation has some one and/or some community behind it that believes there is cause to defend and attribute the obligation. Sanctions can be self imposed and/or imposed by others. Context will typically generate different sorts of sanctions. So for example lying when under oath in court may lead to imprisonment. By contrast, lying to a friend, may well lead to feelings of guilt and shame, and further, if discovered, to loss of friendship and reputation. Responsibility thus has, so far, four key components. They are:

1) A duty or obligation to follow a course of action
2) An ethical framework that underpins the obligation
3) Some one or group being held accountable
4) Through some sort of sanction(s)

On many accounts, the buck stops here. I suggest though that we continue our analysis, for completeness sake. And given too, that as noted above, we are in the midst of all kinds of crises, which are at least in part caused by irresponsible behaviour and/or by an irresponsible orientation, a situation that calls for responsible alternatives.

My objective is to arrive at an understanding of responsibility that is both more dynamic and operational than prevailing accounts. Etymologically, and so in a sense originally, responsibility has two components, that do not appear in the notions of obligation or accountability. They are *response and ability*. So, the term specifically designates the ability to respond or to be responsive[15]. In fact, it would seem that the original meaning has been lost, and substituted by responsibility with a focus on *obligation, accountability, appraisal, and attribution of blame or praise*, to the detriment of responsibility as ability. Indeed, the notion of the capacity to fulfil one's

15. This idea is in part found in Webster's definition 2b: "able to choose between right and wrong".

obligation, and so meet one's responsibility, has all but disappeared. This aspect of the term, however, is, I contend, (still) a key part of the processes involved in meeting responsibilities. Put differently, it is not especially useful to attribute responsibility, if and when a person does not have the ability to meet it.

I thus distinguish responsibility as being articulated along three axes:

(A) An obligation as described above.
(B) The fulfilling of that obligation, producing the desired responsible outcome.
(C) The (three) necessary conditions to meet the obligation (see below).

Clearly, responsibility being attributed to a person (A) does not yet entail that the given obligation will be fulfilled (B). The latter is a supplementary step. I now want to focus more particularly on the third axis (C), the conditions for (B) to hold. Being (held) accountable, at some level at least, presupposes that one is at the very least *capable* of fulfilling the given duty. In fact, for the obligation contained in the responsibility to be met, three *conditions* apply by necessity:

1. Circumstances have to allow for the given obligation to be met.
2. The protagonist has to have the willingness or intention to meet the given obligation, that is, to do so freely or voluntarily.
3. The protagonist has to have the inherent skill or ability to meet the given obligation.

Consequently, for the attribution and carrying out of responsibility, to make full and reasonable sense, all three above conditions need to be taken seriously[16]. On this view, an account of responsibility that is restricted to duty or obligation for which one is held accountable (A), discussions of the possibility of free will, and the ability to accurately apportion blame or praise, even when taken together, fall well short of what is aimed for, when the actual fulfilment of responsible outcomes is the desired result.

16. Whilst it is possible to meet the obligation without intending to, this would count as a chance occurrence, and, as such, it cannot be counted as a necessary condition.

Indeed, to the extent that the objective is typically to obtain responsible outcomes (B) in practice, the three identified conditions (C) clearly constitute a key part of the story. Assuming above conditions 1 and 2 are met, I shall now focus in greater detail on the third condition, that is, on a person's inherent ability to produce responsible outcomes, or on that part, which in fact depends on her.

RESPONSE-ABILITY (THE THIRD CONDITION)

On an approach to responsibility as dynamic or processual, the notion can, we saw, be articulated along three key axes: (A) a duty or obligation for which one is accountable, (B) the successful meeting of the obligation, and (C) the conditions for B to hold. To systematically produce the responsible outcomes that are required of us requires, besides 1) circumstances and 2) intention to succeed, that 3) the protagonist be skilled enough to fulfil the obligation contained in the responsibility attributed to her. Thus, whilst (3) is not in and of its own sufficient to guarantee the outcome contained in a given responsibility, it is a key component towards fulfilling one's duty. Now, in what, more specifically, does such a skill consist? Is it in fact innate and/or to be acquired and/or developed? Let me elaborate.

It is very interesting to find, on conducting a google search for "response ability", there is very little by way of academic references that develop responsibility from the ability perspective. We find responsibility sometimes discussed in these terms on blogs. They are not exactly places that self respecting academics like to refer to, even if increasingly blogs are being set up by academics in parallel with their formal academic website. My concern is in part that the current scholarly approaches to responsibility tend to be predominantly static, and not especially operational. Lay persons' views and contributions resonating with my own may in fact be an indication that a focus on ability is shared by those, less concerned with theory, and more with a desire to see responsibility work in practice.

I suggest that whilst *the skill or ability to meet one's responsibility may require experience, it also requires that the protagonist grasp, in her conception and her actions*[17]*, the correct nature of things, that is, as they truly are, and not as she fantasises, wishes, or distorts*[18] *them, whether these things are persons (including herself), or things such as for instance ecosystems.*

This ability of *non-distortion*, I shall refer to as *realisticness.* The ability is to begin with likely principally contingent on biological factors, given that the foetus comes into the world without having been exposed to much[19] outside influence. Certainly after birth, influences of all sorts interact with the infant's genetic make up to fashion this ability. The very fact that a person is able to cope, and operate in the world is in itself proof of human ability to at some level accurately apprehend and respond to things with realisticness. Indeed, one could not possibly function in the world without taking into account, and without acting according to, its nature (or the nature of things situated in it).

If responsible behaviour is a part of our human potential (most persons are born with a latent disposition to behave responsibly), it is also the case that personal path ways will variously affect each and every one of us in how (well) we develop this capability. Thus, it can be said that individuals who have developed the capacity to behave responsibly have in effect *actualised* a latent potential. As such, they have become capable of responsible action. It is yet a further step for persons to then choose to further actualise their capability into specific responsible moral actions. Put differently, the ability to behave responsibly as a potential may or may not be

17. I differentiate here our conception of things at any point in time, and actions that may result from such a conception. I am well aware, though, that actions can be taken to encompass thought. For a conception is neither static (nothing in the universe is), nor inactive, and as such thought may well be defined as action. This is true especially when we take into account the discovery that the mere fact of the presence of an observer makes a difference to quantum physical outcomes [Bohr 1934].

18. There is no binary here. But the less we distort the better our ability to engage in responsible moral conduct (and the better too we can develop a responsible ethical orientation or virtue).

19. Note that even prior birth, the infant has already been influenced by its environment, the mother's womb, her vibrations, her emotions, her voice, that of the father, and so on.

developed and strengthened, and so actualised, and in turn this skill or capability, may or may not be actualised into certain outcomes, upon fulfilling the particular responsibility being attributed.

We may, of course, on occasion behave in ways that turn out to fulfil the duty contained in our responsibility, without our intending to. But for behaviour to be (counted as) responsible, such outcomes do not in themselves constitute a sufficient criterion. Responsible action should also at some level be intended. Thus, whilst to fulfil one's responsibility yields (morally) *responsible action*, a *responsible person* entails not only that she intends to fulfil, but also regularly fulfils, the obligation(s) contained in the responsibilities attributed to her[20], as well as developing a responsible (ethical) orientation or virtue.

To operationalise the notion of responsibility necessitates moving beyond mere obligation. I have suggested that the capacity to meet given responsibilities has as one of its conditions "*that we grasp, in our conception and our actions, the correct nature of things, that is, as they truly are, and not as we fantasise, wish, or distort them*". The approach to responsibility as processual thus requires us to examine how psychological mind frames affect the ways in which we interpret events and states of affairs. We must, amongst other factors, better understand personal life histories.

Given that to be able to fulfil one's responsibility requires us to accurately capture the nature of things, and in our actions, to take into account this nature, we might argue that a successful ontologist[21] will favourably develop his or her capacity to act responsibly and to be responsible. Indeed, to be aware and take care of the true nature of some (other) person or thing requires a person to view the world as it is, and not as she, or some other person, may fantasise it to be.

20. Whether the intended action needs to be a conscious one, or if indeed unconscious actions can *also* at some level be taken as being intentional, is open to debate, and it is not in fact necessary to take a stance for the purposes of my argument at this point. I shall therefore leave this particular discussion to one side for now.

21. By ontology I mean (the study of) the nature of a domain of reality.

What, though, lies between a person and her perception of reality? A big contender for creating distance between the two, and so for distorting reality and producing inaccurate representations of course is *fear* [Bigo 2008]. There is by now a vast body of literature coming out psychology and psychoanalysis on the subject of fear and distortion. Further contributions exist in economics on the role of "irrational", "emotional", intuitive versus consciously reflected upon, "rational" motives for actions [Lawson 1997; Gintis *et alii* 2003; Kirman and Teschl 2004; Haidt and Graham 2007; Martins 2009; Elster 2010]. Let us examine the fear factor in greater detail.

Fear is a common fate of humanity. We are born undifferentiated from (or one with) the mother, dependant, vulnerable, and mortal. Processes of differentiation and individuation provoke fear and anxiety, as part of the normal course of identity formation. Now, psychoanalytic theory is replete with assessments of how the processes of gaining awareness of (i) difference and (ii) mortality are anxiety provoking, as infants experience a lack of control. Gradually, the original delusion of oneness and control is (often painfully) replaced with a more realistic relation to the world [Mitchell and Black 1995; Tishkomski 2006].

But the process is one that is potentially traumatic and inhibiting [Freud 1933; Klein 1948; Mitchell 2006]. We commonly develop a series of coping mechanisms to defend ourselves in a world that (we on occasion perceive as threatening and which) is unpredictable. Mary Morgan [1995] points out that the difficulty to recognise separateness can lead to *distorted* representations of objects. Such objects are things and persons that act as place holders for that which infants and later adults experience as good or evil, as gratifying or frustrating [22].

As indicated, mainstream western ethical and moral philosophy tends not to focus too much on psychoanalytical considerations,

22. Infants grow up in environments constituted of real and imagined loved persons and objects, "transitional objects", hated and loved ones, that create a psychological landscape, which contribute to fashion personality, fears, hopes, anxieties and neuroses, as they grow up to be adults [Klein 1948; Winnicott 1965].

the deeply engrained unconscious emotional dimensions of human experience that structure the dynamics of the psyche from infancy onwards. And where such aspects are examined in economics, the focus is mostly on experiments that study responses under controlled circumstances [Singer and Fehr 2005]. This literature pays little attention to life histories, including infant anxieties and pleasures, to understand the development of lasting emotional tendencies. This is true even though the latter influence and contribute to fashioning personalities and patterns of behaviour over a life time.

Gradually, experiences that become engrained and have lasting effects on adult behaviour, with ethical and moral implications. Clearly, the more we distort, idealise, devalue, etc., the less we are aware of the actual nature of some self other, person or object. The less too we are consequently able to adopt a responsible orientation, and to successfully meet responsibilities. Whilst punctual experiments may reveal how well the ability has been developed, they constitute the tip of the process of enquiry. Such experiments can be a source for further investigation. Particular psychological life histories must be examined to understand the *causes* of the resulting developments. For upon finding root causes, we are in a position to seek ways of acquiring and/or developing the propensity for realisticness in children and adult citizens [23] as a basis for responsible conduct. I should add that to the extant that identity formation is heavily gendered, distortions will tend to be manifest differently from one sex to another, a point to which I return below [Flax 1990; Bigo 2008].

In terms of consequences, distortion may thus result in two tendencies. At one level, distorted perceptions will typically lead to

23. One can of course run with the conclusion that when agents find themselves in this or that situation, if being stimulated in a given way, they respond in a given way (the if x then y correlation scenario). We can in such cases seek to apply the stimuli that have been identified to induce behaviour. But the risk is 1) that outcomes cannot be replicated across contexts, and 2) that one omits to identify deeply engrained psychic patterns that lie behind the given reactions. Where underlying mechanisms are understood, they can be taken actively into account in aiming to acquire and develop a lasting capacity for realisticness.

our *a priori* ethical frame of reference being itself distorted. Consequently, we will likely be mistaken about which orientations do or do not favour well being, and so misconceive what obligations should be deemed responsible. Second, distortions will typically impair our skill or ability to meet the obligations attached to our responsibilities, however well or ill conceived these obligations may be. Thus whilst, part the focus of my paper is on morality, and in particular on the ability to meet given responsibilities in our actions, it is clearly the case that distortions affects both ethical orientation and moral conduct.

RELATED APPROACHES

Close to my own spirit, moral psychologist, Iris Murdoch [1992], devotes part of her work to an in depth examination of the moral person, her fears and weaknesses, as well as her dreams, "phantasies" (which she takes to be creative, as opposed to fantasies, which she understands to be delusional), and imagination. Her scrutiny of moral character and "moral change" resonates with my own analysis. In her approach to ethics and morality, she too, specifies that moral action hinges on grasping reality, on realisticness as I have termed it. She is not content with a naïve (black box type) understanding of will power and reasoning. She contends that individuals are "free" only in a particular sense. This position can be summarised as follows:

> Murdoch holds freedom and moral change together as internally related concepts integral to the idea of the individual. Both concepts depend on a notion of distance or separation between the grasping, dominating ego and a reality that exceeds the ego. This distance is defined as the reflexive power of moral imagination, the ability of consciousness to escape its own totalizing energies by imagining a good beyond itself. Understood in these terms, freedom is the condition for moral change, since moral change cannot occur without a liberation from egoistic fantasy; conversely, moral change involves the exercise of freedom through the process of unselfing. [Antonaccio 2000, p. 193]

Murdoch's concern is here, like my own, with the "conditions" liable to produce ethical orientation and moral action, conditions, which, she too, associates with psychological make up (she talks of the ego) and realism (rather than egoistic fantasy). Murdoch focuses not so much on responsible conduct, as on moral conduct. We may put the question though as to what distinguishes, if anything, moral and responsible behaviour (principles and orientations). On the face of it, morality is more encompassing than responsibility, but it is hard to ever think of moral conduct as not also being somehow responsible behaviour (and vice versa). Once more, I can unfortunately not, for reasons of space and focus, develop this question here.

A further area has recently emerged in the domain of moral psychology. This area has also distanced itself from naïve (black box) notions of volition and reasoning, as principal vectors to explain and fashion people's ethics and morality. I am referring here to scholarship that has become well known as the *ethics of care*.

The idea of an *ethics of care* originated with Carol Gilligan's [1982] critique of what she termed and contrasted with an *ethics of justice*. The latter, she contends, is based on moral injunctions that do not sufficiently reflect relational contexts. She specifically built on the work of Swiss psychologist, Jean Piaget [1932], and psychologist Lawrence Kohlberg [1966]. Both worked on producing a theory of the development of infant morality. Where Kohlberg focused on adolescent boys, Gilligan criticised him for not paying attention to girls' moral development.

She argues that following gender[24] scripts, girls, and later adult women, tend to be at least partly, when not primarily, concerned with, and care about, the (emotional) effects of their actions on others. In her study of adolescent girls, she observes that they often seek to protect other persons (and their feelings), and that they tend to be in empathy, when deciding on how best to behave. Boys, and later men, in following their gender script, she finds, by

24. Gender can be defined as a system of differentiation and discrimination based on real and/or perceived difference in physical and sexual (or reproductive) attributes.

contrast, tend to place the emphasis on rules or injunctions, where separateness is the primary emotion.

Succinctly, an ethics of care describes (and advocates) an emphasis on empathy in motivating moral decisions and in establishing ethical standards. The limit case, when taken to its logical conclusion, is for empathy to signify "to be one with". This is indeed an aspect of the definition of empathy adopted by the online Webster dictionary[25]:

> 1: the imaginative projection of a subjective state into an object so that the object appears to be infused with it
> 2: the action of understanding, being aware of, being sensitive to, and vicariously experiencing the feelings, thoughts, and experience of another of either the past or present without having the feelings, thoughts, and experience fully communicated in an objectively explicit manner; *also*: the capacity for this.

What transpires from the above is a closeness between 1) my approach to responsibility, 2) Webster's definition of empathy, and 3) the ethics of care and Murdoch's approach to ethics and morality. Indeed, I have argued responsibility requires a "capacity", one that clearly involves "the action of understanding, being aware of, being sensitive to, and vicariously experiencing the feelings, thoughts, and experience of another". It further transpires from the account of the ethics of care that it involves ethical propositions and moral conduct guided by empathy, not least by "being sensitive to, and vicariously experiencing the feelings, thoughts, and experience of another". Clearly, my approach to responsibility shares much with the ethics of care, and with the notion of empathy. Nor are we far from Murdoch's take on morality, for whom, we saw, "imagination" can serve as a vehicle for moral beings to grasp and become "aware" of "reality".

As stated, on my conception of responsibility, I suggest we should actively take into account what inhabits moral persons from the inside, since a prerequisite for responsible action is that it "*requires that we grasp, in our conception and our actions, the accurate nature*

25. http://www.merriam-webster.com/dictionary/empathy.

of things, that is, as these truly are, and not as we fantasise, wish, or distort them". I further note that this propensity for realisticness is one that persons develop over a life time, to different degrees, more or less successfully. Crucially, the propensity varies according to individuals, their personal path ways, and experiences.

To deepen our understanding of responsibility, I have spent time and space discussing some closely related approaches and conceptions. I have done so in order to contextualise my own conception. Conversely, my wish has been to show how the related approaches to ethics and morality (as exemplified by Murdoch and Gilligan) can in many ways be seen as centrally addressing the question of responsibility. Below, I draw out some of the consequences that ensue from the approach to responsibility adopted in this paper. In particular, I examine possible leverages to creating generations of more responsible citizens?

RESPONSIBLE CITIZENS

I have argued that responsibility, in particular responsible conduct, constructs itself in a relation between the self and that, which is different from us: others (or other things). Indeed, differences between ourselves, our desires, and (those of) others, are often wished or fantasised away. To be responsible (to systematically behave responsibly) requires realisticness, that is, to grasp the nature of things without (too much) distortion.

Now, because relationships between sexes are the most universal source of difference in the social realm, they constitute a potential *space* for fashioning our ability to engage in responsible conduct. Gender differences and gender relations are in fact an essential source of identity in any society. We are before all else identified as male or female, and considerable confusion ensues if a particular individual is not clearly identifiable as belonging to either sex [26]. Furhter, where patriarchal norms, values, and institu-

26. Certainly, in most western nations operations are performed at birth on infants whose their sexual organs do not fit into the male or female category.

tions are operational, the feminine is systematically cast as inferior to the masculine. Indeed, gender relations are often marked by inequality, which on many counts is not a morally responsible outcome.

There are, of course, plenty of other spaces in which differences result in expressions of intolerance. Take cultural and religious differences and intolerances for example. We thus observe fear of difference being played out in intimate family contexts, as well as very widely in the international political arena. But gender relations, as well as being most universal, and permeating all social relations, profoundly affect child development and identity formation. As such, they deserve special attention.

Now, part of the explanation for the gender hierarchy is that processes of differentiation and individuation often generate *fear*. For the latter typically produces intolerance of what is other and different from us, or of what is beyond our control, as well as having power over us (in the first instance this other is synonymous with the mother or prime carer). Indeed, one, if not the root cause for the various manifestations of intolerance, we noted, is fear, a primal fear of loosing one's sense of identity. Thus to learn to tolerate and accept each other across gender differences, means in conjunction that we develop our ability to take on board differences, as they are and not we wish and distort them. It is in this way that gender relations can be a space in and through which we can develop our *realisticness*, and so one of the conditions for being able to adopt morally responsible conduct, and ethical orientations.

Achieving fundamental change in gender stereotypes likely entails new more gender neutral family configurations, with truly shared parenting responsibilities, on the one hand. On the other, such transformation requires societal, especially professional attitudinal and organisational changes, capable of espousing both parents in their roles as carers. Such shifts in attitude are advocated by certain militants in favour of incorporating caring responsibilities in definitions of citizenship [Sevenhuijsen 1998]. Feminist economists have also long argued that we should value care, and balance care responsibilities between the sexes, as capitalism and patriarchy free ride on women's free and/or cheap reproductive labour [Beneria 1979; England *et alii* 2002; Elson 2006; Bigo and Gray 2009].

Our *positions* as parents, professionals, neighbours, voters, etc., occupied in varying contexts further influence us when developing our gender references. Breaking the mould of caring responsibilities, by involving men on a par with women in the vast quantities of care labour performed, would of course radically change the way every other sphere of human activity is meted out. And the more people, across strata, are widely exposed to and gain awareness of a wide range of ideas, situations, environments, and practices, the more likely our citizens will be able to produce appropriate responses, adopting a responsible (ethical) orientation, and engaging in responsible (moral) behaviour.

A complementary form of action to reduce gender stereotypes is to influence gender norms and practices in the public and/or collective sphere, by, for example, introducing quotas for women's equal representation in governmental spheres, and in top positions more generally. One can further aim to systematically educate and inform the population so as to promote their ability to discern, whilst diminishing their tendency to fearfully and/or ignorantly distort.

Processes of transformation in gender norms and relations will likely require time. Families can be very modern and egalitarian in trying to raise their sons and daughters in much the same way. Traditional patterns, however, permeate parents' emotions, thoughts and actions, very often without their noticing. In addition, children soon come in contact with all sorts of individuals, and find themselves in all kinds of contexts, which bring their own gender norms. Thus whilst parents may seek to break certain gender patterns in how they raise their children, in parallel, these same norms will in great part be tacitly reproduced. The process of change is thus necessarily iterative, and very often slow.

I suggest responsible behaviour further entails that we strike a balance between following *a priori* (abstract) ethical principles, and *a posteriori* adopting context specific moral (decisions and) behaviour. We saw there to be an observed tendency for men to be favour specific *a priori* rules, and for women to *a posteriori* relational context dependant decision making.

A word of caution is warranted here. Indeed, we should avoid amalgamating men with *a prioriness*, and vice versa. For, in their own way, women can be just as systematically *a priori*. Indeed, wittingly or not systematically privileging empathy and relational context has a form of *a prioriness* to it, and constitutes an ethical orientation of its own. It is simply a principle that dictates that in practice context should determine which particular way to best (morally) behave, as well as suggesting that care and empathy should motivate one's ethical orientation.

Once more, the ability to behave responsibly typically hinges on finding a balance between the two tendencies, *a priori* rules, and *a posteriori* input given by (relational) context. Consequently, our veering away from current gender stereotypes should also on this count be, on the face of it, a constructive move.

In sum, generations of responsible citizens will very possibly (when not necessarily) consist of individuals that have been able to individuate and develop their personality, without systematically and defensively distorting the world. To favour realisticness, in one's orientation and in carrying out obligations, requires for children to be brought up in relatively emotionally secure environments. Further, being and acting responsibly (producing responsible orientations and effectively carrying out moral responsibilities) typically requires that we take into account sets of abstract principles, as well as specific relational contexts. Individuals would on this view benefit from moving away from stereotypical gender orientation and behaviour, and so in the end also from ethical and moral stereotypical versions of responsibility.

Final comments

My objective has been to emphasise the need to flesh out the concept of responsibility, in a world that fails so acutely in its ability to *respond* to crises of all sorts. The global financial crisis appears at a time when there is, in conjunction, a global crisis in care. This hardly seems to be a coincidence. Indeed, the two are no doubt related. If care has anything to do with ethics and morality, then the crisis in the provision of care arguably extends to a crisis in governance and an inability to meet some of society's key challenges. Such ineptitude is seemingly symptomatic of societies that fail to value empathy.

In any case, if crises are anything to go by, contemporary societies do not do well by way of responsible outcomes. I have suggested this is at least in part due to a lack of ability and so failure to adopt an ethical orientation, as well as a lack of skill or ability to act responsibly, morally. In this context, how satisfied should we be with the assertions that one should apply rules of governance to harness financial systems gone wild? I seriously contend that it is both inadequate and insufficient to concentrate on *rules* of governance to generate (morally) responsible actions. I have thus further suggested that we do more in the face of disastrous financial abuses than merely repeatedly declare that we *should* behave more responsibly, argue whether we are free or determined in our actions, and whether we can 'objectively' apportion blame or praise. Perhaps we are ready to take on a different, more dynamic notion of responsibility.

I have argued in this paper that we can and should dig deeper and further, to better understand responsibility. I have advanced an understanding of the notion as processual or dynamic that can be contrasted with the traditional more static definitions. In my approach, I note that responsibility involves three key dimensions: duty, outcomes, and conditions of fulfilment. We saw, for obligations contained in the responsibilities to be met, three *conditions* apply by necessity: circumstances must not obstruct, the agent should have the intention to oblige (unless we have a chance occurrence), and the agent should have a certain ability for realisticness.

We saw too that, literally, responsibility is "the ability to respond". Presently, it makes more sense of course to speak of the widespread *inability* to respond. If responsibility's etymology reminds us that the notion of responsibility is associated with a capacity of response, this aspect of responsibility seems to be lost both in practice and theory. Indeed, individuals seem to inadequately develop their capacity to be responsive, and so to behave responsibly. It is this aspect of the term responsibility as, "response ability", that I have addressed with some urgency in my paper.

Gender norms and relations are strong candidates for us to examine, and potentially work on, our ability for being realistic about things we wish were different. As such, I have argued that they constitute an important potential vector for change, one that can support emancipatory initiatives in favour of well being.

In sum, the presence of responsibility presupposes a human capacity to behave responsibly that 1) individuals successfully develop to different degrees, and which 2) may or may not be manifest in behaviour. This capacity is best understood as emerging with the development of identity, as we (seek to) overcome our fear of otherness or difference. Specifically, the ability to respond to obligations involves developing an ability to be realistic (or not to distort). I have attempted in this paper to shed light on some of the many complex issues in play, which are very often and surprisingly neglected, in discussions of governance and responsibility.

Being explicit – about the categories ethics and morality, the place of realism, relativism, the place of free will, will power and determinism in one's conception of human behaviour – is key when seeking to solve the responsibility "puzzle". As well as revisiting these central issues, I have developed an approach to responsibility as dynamic, one that encompasses, yet goes further than, the habitual themes discussed in theories of responsibility. My objective has been to propose a new and hopefully helpful understanding of responsibility, one that examines the processes whereby the agent acquires the realisticness that underpins the *ability* to *respond* successfully to her obligations. For meeting the challenges of contemporary society is a dream that no doubt requires a fair doses of realisticness.

References

ALKIRE S., 2005, "Capability and Functionings: Definition and Justification", in *Briefing Notes: Human Development and Capability Association*, Havard, Havard isites, online at: isites.harvard.edu/fs/docs/icb.topic711934.files/AlkireCV08.pdf

ANTONACCIO M., 2000, *Picturing the Human: The Moral Thought of Iris Murdoch*, Oxford-New York, Oxford University Press.

APTER T., 2008, *The Sister Knot: Why We Fight, Why We're Jealous and Why We'll Love Each Other No Matter What*, New York, W.W. Norton.

BENERIA L., 1979, "Reproduction, Production and the Sexual Division of Labour", *Cambridge Journal of Economics*, 3(3), p. 203-225.

BIGO V., 2008, "Explaining Modern Economics (as a Microcosm of Society)", *Cambridge Journal of Economics*, 32(4), p. 527-554.

— and MIA G., 2009, "Constructing Care: For Love or Money", *Revue de Philosophie Économique*, 10(1), *Enjeux éthiques en économie de la santé*, p. 103-124.

BOHR N., 1934, *Atomic Theory and Description of Nature*, Cambridge, Cambridge University Press.

BORDO R.S., 1987, *The Flight to Objectivity: Essays on Cartesianism and Culture*, New York, State University of New York Press.

ELSON D., 2006, *Budgeting for Women's Rights: Monitoring Government Budgets for Compliance with Cedaw*, New York, UNIFEM.

ELSTER J., 2010, "The Self-Poisoning of the Mind", *Philosophical Transactions of the Royal Society*, 365 January, Trans. R. Soc. B 27(1538), p. 221-226.

ENGLAND P., BUDIG M. and FOLBRE N., 2002, "Wages of Virtue: The Relative Pay of Care Work", in *Social Problems*, vol. 49, n° 4, p. 455-473.

FLAX J., 1990, *Thinking Fragments: Psychoanalysis, Feminism, and Postmodernism in the Contemporary West*, Berkeley-Los Angeles-Oxford, University of California Press.

FREUD S., 1933, "New Introductory Lectures on Psycho-Analysis", in *Standard Edition*, 22, p. 5-182.

GILLIGAN C., 1982, *In a Different Voice: Psychological Theory and Women's Development*, Cambridge (Mass.), Harvard University Press.

GINTIS H., BOWLES S., BOYD R. and FEHR E., 2003, "Explaining Altruistic Behavior in Humans", *Evolution and Human Behavior*, vol. 24, p. 153-172.

HAIDT J. and JESSE G., 2007, "When Morality Opposes Justice: Conservatives Have Moral Intuitions That Liberals May Not Recognize", *Social Justice Research*, vol. 20, p. 98-116.

KIRMAN A. and TESCHL M., 2004, "On the Emergence of Economic Identity", *Revue de Philosophique Économique*, 9(1), p. 59-86.

KLEIN M., 1948, "A Contribution to the Theory of Anxiety and Guilt", *International Journal of Psychoanalysis*, vol. 29, p. 113-123.

KOHLBERG L.A., 1966, "A Cognitive-Developmental Analysis of Children's Sex Role Concepts and Attitudes", *in* E.E. Maccoby (ed.), *The Development of Sex Differences*, Stanford, Stanford University Press, p. 82-173.

LAWSON T., 1997, *Economics and Reality*, London, Routledge.

– 2000, "Evaluating Trust, Competition and Co-Operation", in *Competition, Trust and Co-Operation – a Comparative Study*, Y. Shionoya and K. Yagi (eds.), New York-Berlin-Tokyo, Springer Verlag.

MARTINS N., 2009, "Neuroeconomics, Rationality And Preference Formation: Methodological: Implications for Economic Theory", in *The Capabilities Conference*, Oxford.

MITCHELL J., 2000, *Mad Men and Medusas: Reclaiming Hysteria and the Effects of Sibling Relations on the Human Condition*, London, Allen Lane and Penguin Book.

MITCHELL S.A. and BLACK M.J., 1995, *Freud and Beyond: A History of Modern Psychoanalytic Thought*, New York (NY), Basic Books.

MOORE G.E., 1903, *Principia Ethica*, Cambridge, Cambridge University Press.

MORGAN M., 1995, "The Projective Gridlock: A Form of Projective Identification in Couple Relationships", *in* S. Ruszczynski and J. Fisher (eds.), *Intrusiveness and Intimacy in the Couple*, London, Karnac, p. 33-48.

MURDOCH I., 1992, *Metaphysics as a Guide to Morals*, New York, Penguin.

NUSSBAUM M.C., 1995, "Human Capabilities, Female Human Beings", *in* M.C. Nussbaum and J. Glover (eds.), *Women, Culture, and Development: A Study of Human Capabilities*, Oxford, Clarendon Press.

PIAGET J., 1932, *The Moral Judgment of the Child*, New York, Harcourt.

SEN A., 1982, *Poverty and Famines: An Essay on Entitlements and Deprivation*, Oxford, Clarendon Press.

SEVENHUIJSEN S., 1998, *Citizenship and the Ethics of Care: Feminist Considerations on Justice, Morality and Politics*, London, Routledge.

SHIVA V., 1989, *Staying Alive*, London, Zed.

SINGER T. and Fehr E., 2005, "The Neuroeconomics of Mind Reading and Empathy", *American Economic Review*, vol. 95, p. 340-345.

STRAWSON P., 1962, "Freedom and Resentment", *Proceedings of the British Academy*, p. 481-25.

TISHKOWSKI D., 2006, "A Brief History of Psychoanalytical Thought: Freud and His Psychoanlytical Innovators", online at: http://clearinghouse.missouriwestern.edu/manuscripts/565.asp

WINNICOTT D., 1965, "Failure of Expectable Environment on Child's Mental Functioning", *International Journal of Psychoanalysis*, vol. 46, p. 81-87.

DO MARKETS FOSTER SELFISHNESS?

ALAN KIRMAN AND MIRIAM TESCHL*

Résumé

L'agent économique est souvent par définition considéré comme un pur égoïste. Plus encore, son utilité est définie sur ce qu'il consomme et elle est considérée comme monotone – ce que nous appelons être « égoïste ». Dans cet article, nous nous intéressons à l'hypothèse selon laquelle le marché conduit les individus à être égoïstes. Nous avançons tout d'abord que la théorie économique n'est pas limitée à considérer des agents économiques égoïstes mais qui peuvent également faire des choix fondés sur d'autres motivations, par exemple des agents qui ont des préférences altruistes envers les autres. Dans une deuxième partie de cet article, nous discutons plusieurs expériences en économie qui traitent des conditions dans lesquelles les préférences altruistes peuvent se manifester. Dans ce contexte, nous discutons en particulier trois aspects: la concurrence, la complétude des contrats et la différence entre l'argent gagnée et l'argent inattendue (ou « windfall money »). Ces trois facteurs, sous des circonstances particulières, semblent contribuer à l'observation de comportements plus égoïstes. Nous concluons que le fait de gagner de l'argent par sa propre activité et la responsabilité jouent un rôle spécifique dans la prévalence des comportement égoistes.

Mots clés : *agent économique, égoïsme, préférences altruistes, gift exchange game, concurrence, monnaie gagnée* vs *monnaie inattendue*

Abstract

The economic agent is almost by definition considered to be purely self-interested. But even more than this, his utility is defined over what he consumes and in this he is monotonic. We

* A. Kirman: GREQAM, University Paul Cézanne, EHESS, IUF (France), kirman@univmed.fr; M. Teschl: Department of Economics, University of Vienna (Austria), miriam.teschl@univie.ac.at.

refer to this as being "selfish". In this paper we investigate the claim that markets make people selfish. We first argue that economic theory allows us to consider economic agents who make choices on the basis of motivations other than just selfishness, for example agents who have other-regarding preferences. In the second part of the paper, we discuss a number of economic experiments that deal with the conditions under which in a market situation other-regarding behaviour does manifest itself. In this context we discuss three aspects, namely competition, the completeness of contracts and the difference between earned money and windfall gains. All these three factors, under particular circumstances seem to contribute to more selfish behaviour. We conclude that earned money and responsibility play a particular role in determining the prevalence of selfish behaviour.
Keywords: economic agent, selfishness, other-regarding preferences, gift exchange game, competition, earned money *vs* windfall money

JEL Classification: D10, D31, D64

1. Introduction

What influence do markets have on the objectives that individuals pursue? In economic theory, the answer would seem to be not much. A market is simply the place where people, who are typically self-interested, meet to barter and to exchange, to sell those things or services they have produced or own, and to buy those things and services that they most cherish given their budget constraint. Self-interest here is used in a very narrow sense which we will refer to in this paper as "selfishness" or as "pure" self-interest. Edgeworth [1881] said, "The first principle of economics is that every agent is actuated only by self-interest" [p. 16]. But as John Broome [1999] points out, whilst in Edgeworth's time self-interest could be equated with selfishness in our sense, Lionel Robbins [1984] could already say, "So far as we are concerned our economic subjects can be pure egoists, pure altruists, pure ascetics, pure sensualists or – what is more likely – bundles of all these impulses" [p. 95]. Self-interest defined as simply being consistent with the axioms we impose becomes tautological. However, even if we make the distinction, as we do between self-interested and selfish, there are still arguments to support the idea that people can be purely selfish and their behaviour still be consistent with the social interest. As Adam Smith already pointed out with his butcher, brewer and baker example, the whole of society will be made better off as the unintentional result of the butcher, brewer and baker's selfish behaviour. Another argument is that of course, if people were not selfish, they could be exploited in several ways by those who were selfish and, contrary to what one may have thought, they may end up worse in terms of their more general utility function than if they simply acted selfishly. This would be a sort of natural selection answer to our original question, which may be in the mind of many, including many economists, when they consider the influence markets as institutions may have on the behaviour of people. That is, to survive in a market environment people are driven to be purely selfish. This is, of course, questionable and is at the heart of the issues that we address in this paper. Indeed, many actually think that other social institutions, such as for example the family, where personal relations – contrary to markets – are dominant, influence the individual in such a way that they become other-regarding and not only selfish. This is because relations outside the market are typically social relations, whilst there are not in the market. Bruni and Sugden [2008] summarise this nicely when they say:

> Smith's account of the butcher, the brewer and the baker, is the idea that trading partners are normally indifferent to one another's interests, and that this indifference is not a matter for moral criticism: in David Gauthier's [1986, p. 84] phrase, a perfectly competitive market would be a 'morally free zone, a zone in which the constraints of morality would have no place'. The beneficial consequences of markets – their tendency to promote the 'wealth of nations' – are unintended by-products of individuals' pursuit of their private interests; they play no essential role in those individuals' own understandings of what they are doing. Thus, market relationships are not in any real sense social. Or, saying the same thing the other way round, if there is a realm of genuine social relationships, it exists outside the market, and is characterized by forms of mutual concern that are not found in markets. [p. 38].

What if this is not the case? Another way to pose the problem would be to say that people have various motivations which can be either self-regarding or other-regarding and it is the context, including the market itself, that determines to what extent individuals act selfishly. This, at least, will be the hypothesis of this paper.

Samuel Bowles [1998] analyses a very similar hypothesis and talks of the "construal effect" of markets to distinguish it from a related but milder concept known in economics, which is the "framing effect" [p. 87]. His view is that markets construct people's preferences; hence people have endogenous preferences that emerge with the context in which they interact. In this article, we take up the view of the construal effect and consider some particular aspects of the "market" that may influence people's behaviour. In order to see what the contextual influence of markets is we analyse a number of economic experiments that were set up to test for the existence of people's other-regarding behaviour and whether such behaviour would be consistent with the existence of other-regarding or social preferences. What are the characteristic of market situations which might be influential? One aspect is competition. Competition is of course thought of as being a key feature of markets. Typical market experiments generally show that other-regarding behaviour is not sustainable because with competition, behaviour converges quickly to the equilibrium predicted by standard economic theory that relies on a selfish agent. However, a number of gift exchange games, initiated in particular by Fehr *et alii* [1993] have shown that even with competition, this equilibrium may not be achieved. One has to be careful though since the equilibrium is defined in terms of the monetary pay-offs which may not correspond to the utility of those pay-offs. So what may emerge is an equilibrium corresponding to the true utility function which may not correspond simply to the monetary pay-offs. However, rather than reasoning in terms of alternative utility functions it can also be argued that in many circumstances contracts are not complete and that is this that prevents the standard equilibrium being achieved. When contracts are incomplete informal cooperative arrangements may replace more formal agreements. Indeed, it is a relatively common view in economics nowadays, expressed by Bowles himself and other people, that the incompleteness of contracts makes people adhere to social norms and other mechanisms that make the outcome deviate from the selfish outcome, or make outcomes possible that otherwise would not have come about under the assumption of pure selfishness. However, whilst these results seem to hold in the laboratory, they may not necessarily hold in the field. Indeed, a field experiment conducted by List [2006] that implements the same conditions as the gift exchange model but in a "real" sports card market shows, to the contrary, that the incompleteness of markets does not foster cooperative, or other-regarding behaviour.

The difference between the laboratory experiments and the field experiment in the context of gift exchange games, we suggest here, is that in the laboratory, people only have to deal with windfall money, whilst in the field they deal with earned money. It is also true that effort expended to earn the money that is in play does not figure in any of these experiments. In general, when people participate in markets they are using resources which they have earned and which they have not simply acquired as a windfall. Starting with Cherry *et alii* [2002], it has been shown that the difference between windfall and earned money has a substantial impact on other-regarding behaviour: in dictator games in which the dictator earns the money through effort, the dictator is considerably less likely to give than in games with windfall money. This would suggest that in market situations one is less likely to observe other regarding behaviour. Nevertheless, other games have shown that while the earned money effect always has a strong impact on other-regarding behaviour, it does not completely rule out the existence of social preferences. This is especially the case if information is given about who receives the money and whether for example they did or did not have the chance to earn any money and thus exerted some effort or did not have the chance to do so, or whether they had the chance but did not take it and hence did not invest any effort. This insight might lead one to conclude that what seems to determine whether people's behaviour is other-regarding or not is the effort made by individuals themselves and observed or perceived by others. The notion that effort has been furnished involves the idea of responsibility. Effort and responsibility are values that seem to be particularly relevant in market situations, in comparison to values that may be important in other institutions. It is, however, far from being etablished that this determines if people are or are not other-regarding and a great deal of experimental work needs to be done to see if there is a clear link here.

However, if it is the case that the economic agent per se is not selfish, but only becomes so through market interaction, is it not the case then that the whole theoretical construction of the economic agent who maximises his utility function is wrong? We will argue that this is not the case and that such an idea reflects a fundamental misunderstanding of economic theory. A simple summary of the economic theory of the individual is that he makes the best choice available to him. Economic theory does not say why he does so but simply imposes consistency conditions on his choices. What can be thought of, and is often expressed as, the standard view of a purely selfish agent may persist simply because it is has become a norm and not for any logical or scientific reasons. Yet nothing in theory says that the economic agent needs to behave this way, that is to confine his interests to purely personal variables. The assumption of purely selfish behaviour has led to many interesting insights and was certainly a useful assumption in many market situations, but as already mentioned, economists from at least Robbins onwards have argued that economic theory has the tools to incorporate behaviour that is also based on other motivations than selfishness.

This paper is organised as follows. Section 2 goes back to the "roots" of the economic agent and shows that the theoretical construction of the economic agent does not imply that he or she is selfish. Section 3 then reviews the experimental evidence that revealed some discrepancies with the predictions of the purely selfish model and discusses in particular the effect of competition, incomplete contracts, earned money and effort on the economic agent's behaviour. Section 4 concludes by pointing out that the view that market influences people's behaviour may be less relevant if one takes an evolutionary approach to human behaviour. In this case, markets play only a minor role in the forging of survival strategies and context as such would matter much less than the natural selection process.

2. THE ECONOMIC AGENT'S MOTIVES

Self-interest and in its strongest form, that of selfishness, is a key idea in economics. It is still widely held that the economic agent acts to fulfil as best as possible his selfish interests. In many economics papers the standard behaviour of the economic agent is said to rely on the "self-interest hypothesis" [*e.g.* Fehr and Schmidt 1999; Frey and Meier 2004], but again by this is meant the assumption that the economic agent is maximising his material self-interest, in the sense that he is "greedy" [*e.g.* Sobel 2009], filling his pockets with more money rather than less. Some go even so far as to attribute a "self-interest axiom" to the behavioural foundations of the economic agent [*e.g.* Henrich *et alii* 2005; Meier 2007]. If one takes the analysis of individual behaviour at its most basic level the assumption of monotonicity of preferences can be thought of as being akin to selfishness. This also explains why it is not uncommon to equate rational behaviour in economics to selfish behaviour.

There is now considerable experimental evidence that shows that subjects are not only guided by selfishness [for overviews see *e.g.* Ledyard 1995; Camerer 2003]. Andreoni and Miller [2002] have provided evidence that people engaging in altruistic behaviour satisfy the general axiom of revealed preferences (GARP) thus showing that behaviour other than that which is selfish is also perfectly rational according to standard definitions of rationality in economics. However, even before experimental and behavioural economics became such a prominent field within economics, several theoretical economists have pointed out that the narrowly defined self-interest hypothesis is erroneous, not only because people may behave in different ways and not necessarily selfishly, but also because the standard tools of economics actually allow us to take full account of behaviour that is not based on pure self-interest [Binmore 2009; Sobel 2009]. One of the most famous defenders of the economic agent acting on a multitude of motives, including norms, preferences, and other principles, is Amartya Sen, who, as is well known, referred to the "egoistic" economic agent as a "rational fool", not because it would be foolish to be selfish, but because it would be foolish to think that the economic agent only knows to behave selfishly [Sen 1977]. Sen is probably also one of the economists who have given most conceptual structure to the different forms of behaviour of which the economic agent is capable [*e.g.* Sen 1985, 1997, 2002]. For example, Sen [1985] has specified different degrees of "privateness" of individual orderings, which can range from purely self-centred welfare concerns to the pursuit of different goals that go far beyond one's one personal welfare. Hence, what is at issue is not the existence of a utility function but the nature of the space over which it is defined.

Despite these influential contributions, the standard view of the economic agent still has it that he is acting in a purely "self-interested" way. It is here where the distinction between self-interest and selfishness becomes useful. Many refer to "self-interest" and mean selfishness, but not always. The idea that agents act in their own self interest may actually cause confusion because it can be interpreted in different ways, which may or may not include altruistic or other-regarding aspects. First, (1) self-interest can be purely "self-centred" in the sense that a person is simply satisfying his own personal preferences, independent of other people's preferences. As observed above, Sen would refer to this as self-centred welfare concerns. This is what we refer to as "selfish". However, a person can also fulfil his self-interest and take account of other people's interests. Here, several cases are possible: (2a) a person may satisfy another person's interest purely for strategic reasons. By strategic reasons it is meant that this person is in fine *only* satisfying his own selfish interests and acts *nobly* towards someone else only because of this. Sen referred to this as "strategic nobility" [1997] [1]. For example, a person wants to be known to be a gene-

1. Sometimes this is also referred to as "extended self-interest" [Meier 2007].

rous person and therefore gives to charity. What is at issue here is reputation. Reputation concerns may incite the economic agent to act in a way that may be other-regarding, but that is still perfectly explicable on the basis of purely self-centred preferences. However, (2b) a person can also genuinely be interested in the wellbeing or advantage of another person. If the person likes to see another person's preferences satisfied, either through his own doing but also more generally, this is typically considered to be an act of self-interest because it is said to promote the agent's welfare at the same time as the welfare of the other person. Sen [1977] famously referred to this form of behaviour as acting out of sympathy with someone. The only point of controversy as to whether something can be counted as self-interest or not is when a person does something for another person which seems to be against their own interest. For example, consider a person who likes giving to another person at the expense of his own consumption. Two interpretations are possible. One (3a) is that the person acts out of principles, whether they are psychologically, socially or even morally determined and which may exist alongside any purely selfish preferences. For example, he may be profoundly against inequality which he considers to be unjust or he may follow particular rules of conduct and therefore always leave the larger piece of cake to the other person. This behaviour is then defined as altruistic or other-regarding to differentiate it from behaviour on the basis of pure self-interest. Sen [1977] would refer to this as acting out of commitment[2]. The other interpretation (3b) is that given that the person has chosen to give to someone else rather than to consume himself, he must still prefer, for whatever reason, this situation to the other one. Hence, *in fine*, this must be better for him and therefore it is his self-interest that makes him act in this way. Hence the view here is that *any* action is *necessarily* a self-

2. To be precise, for Sen [1977] to act out of commitment, it is sufficient that the expected welfare for a person from that action is decreasing. This means that the increase or the expected increase in welfare is not the reason why a person does choose a particular action or behaviour. It may however be the case that for certain actions, whether the person acts out of commitment and or with the aim to increase welfare, both motivations give the same outcome.

interested one. Here we return to the central idea in economic theory, that choices simply reflect a particular person's preferences.

While this last view (3b) is very common among economists [and external critics of economics too], other economists stress the falsity of it. In fact, Binmore [2009] writes:

> It isn't true that it is axiomatic in economic theory that people are selfish. I suspect that this widespread misunderstanding arises because people think that rational agents must act out of self-interest because they maximize their own utility functions rather than some social objective function. [p. 21]

Sen [2002] points out two other difficulties that arise if every individual choice is seen as an expression of pure self-interest. One is related to the fact that rationality depends on freedom, the very idea that is considered to be at the basis not only of a market economy, but also of the power the economic agent has in that very same market, incorporated in the idea of consumer sovereignty (*i.e.* the agent knows best what is "best" for him):

> […] the concept of rationality must accommodate the diversity of reasons that may sensibly motivate choice. To deny that accommodation in favor of conformity with some preselected mechanical axioms [in the form of alleged requirements of "internal consistency of choice"], or with some prespecified "appropriate" motivation [such as the canonical selection of "self-interest maximization" as an exclusive guide, rejecting all other concerns that people have] would involve, in effect, a basic denial of *freedom of thought*. [p. 5, italics in the original]

The second issue that Sen stresses is the fact that the idea of an all-dominant self-interest comes along with the assumption of an "all-purpose ordering" [Sen 2002, p. 7]. The assumption in economic rational choice theory is that the economic agent acts on the basis of an all-things-considered preference ordering. This means that all the different motives the agent may have had are regarded as being incorporated into one single preference ordering on the basis of which the agent henceforth makes his choices. The overarching ordering-principle is then considered to define an agent's self-interest. It is well known that without such a well-behaved preference ordering, it may be impossible to construct a utility function that the agent is supposed to maximise. Traditional economic rational choice theory does not question the possibility of actually having an all-things-considered preference ordering; it simply starts from the assumption that there is one. Indeed, many models begin by specoifying from the outset, a specific utility function without necessarily looking into the axioms on preferences that the economic agent would need to fulfil in order to be able to have such a utility function. Such a presupposed utility function may actually contain several motives other than narrowly defined self-interest [such as *e.g.* a social identity component as in Akerlof and Kranton [2000] which means that agents are willing to adhere to the characteristics of the group to which they belong], the point is however that these different motives lead to choices and arbitrages which assumed to be consistent with writing an overall utility function. This is usually done either by attributing a particular weight to each of the motivations, or by assuming that some "psychic gains" or "costs" arise if the agents does or does not comply with either the norm following (the agent may feel "guilty") or with their self-interest. If the utlility function is assumed to be additively separable in this way it has been argued that this amounts, in principle, to assume some form of cardinalisation in order to resolve the puzzle of the comparability of utilities that arise from different motives. Whatever the case, the overall utility function is typically taken to be synonymous with that individual's self-interest.

What if the overarching ordering-principle was not self-interest? Then another problem would arise to which Sen, again, pointed out as early as 1973. The predominant view, as we have observed, in economics is that observed choices reveal a person's preferences. The idea is that what the person chooses must be best for her. However, what is "best" for her stands for two things at the same time: it says first that it is what the person "prefers", that is, between two alternatives, which is chosen. But it is also considered to be an expression of that person's welfare. It is not clear that what is chosen is tautologically equivalent to what increases welfare as it is usually understood. Motives of choice other than pure self-interest "drive" as Sen would say, "a wedge between choice and welfare" [Sen 1973, p. 259]. "Preference can be defined in such a way as to preserve its correspondence with choice, or defined so as to keep it in line with welfare as seen by the person in question, but it is not in general possible to guarantee both simultaneously" [*ibid.*]. To repeat, the argument is simply is that any choice that is not based on pure self-interest may not necessarily lead to something that increases a person's welfare. To the contrary, as we have seen above, truly altruistic acts are considered to be actions that may for example reduce the consumption of a person for the sake of increasing it for another person. This situation may be preferred to a situation in which the person increases her own consumption, but it may not make her better off in a more restricted sense. Especially not if one is unwilling to accept that the "warm glow" (or some psychic gain) that may arise from such an action is anything more than an arbitrary way of explaining behavioural discrepancies. Or consider norm-following: a young girl may agree to marry the man her parents have chosen for her, but this choice may not necessarily increase her welfare, indeed the result may be quite to the contrary. Or consider in this light the individual who consents to sacrifice a kidney for a transplant. To what extent has this benevolent but irreversible act increased their welfare?

Hence, it seems that the real issue is not whether or not the economic agent is selfish, as some experimental and behavioural economists have been eager to point out, but under what conditions the agent will behave in, what can be interpreted as a selfish way. While a majority of economists certainly do consider selfishness as the main motivation of the economic agent, it is not true that it is an axiomatic foundation of behaviour. For a number of economists, there has never been a doubt that selfishness may just be one of many motives that prompt a choice of the economic agent. The next important issue then seems to be how to assess welfare if behavioural motives are other than selfishness or even favour some general self-interest. This issue has not yet been taken up widely in experimental studies. There are however several theoretical propositions that suggest expanding the limited space over which preference space are defined and incorporating aspects of, for example, equality of opportunity instead, or turn to the measurement of well-being in terms of functionings and capabilities, as Sen [*e.g.* 1999] has proposed. In the rest of this paper, we will not look further into the question of welfare, but consider some experimental evidence that may suggest under what conditions people have the tendency to act in a more selfish way and whether this can tell us something about particular aspects of the market that influences people's behaviour in that sense.

3. Competition, complete contracts and earned money – Do they make the economic agent more selfish?

Almost 20 years ago, Roth *et alii* [1991] studied bargaining and market behaviour in Jerusalem, Ljubljana, Pittsburgh and Tokyo. The bargaining situation was based on a two-person ultimatum game in which a proposer makes a proposal of how to divide 10 dollars and the responder either accepts or rejects the offer. If he accepts, both of them get the proposed amounts, if he rejects, both of them get nothing. The market treatment implied that instead of one proposer, several "buyers" made price offers of which the highest was either accepted or rejected by the responder, a single seller. If the seller accepts, he earns the highest prices offered, and the buyer who made the offer received the difference between the value of the object and the price he offered, all other buyers get zero. If the seller rejects the offer, nobody gets anything. They find that independently of where they conducted the experiment, in the market treatment the outcome converged quickly to the equilibrium in which one side [here the seller] reaps all the benefits, whilst in the bargaining treatment, this equilibrium was not reached. The results of the market behaviour were thus in line with other observations from experimental markets which all have remarkable convergence properties [*e.g.* Smith 1962; Davis and Holt 1993]. The interesting point here however is the difference between market behaviour and bargaining behaviour

– non-market interaction allows for other-regarding preferences, whilst markets with competition, here among buyers, do not.

Fischbacher, Fong and Fehr [2009] had a similar result with responder competition in an ultimatum game. The increase in competition between responders decreased the share the responder would get. The introduction of already one additional responder decreased the responder's average share of the pie from 42 to roughly 20 percent. However, as also Fehr and Fischbacher [2002] note, this does not mean that markets necessarily turn other-regarding people into selfish people[3]. It rather suggests that competition does not allow for another "preference" of people to manifest itself. They refer to this "other" preference as reciprocity. Reciprocity is a motive "revealed" by experimental economists and that may be in conflict with selfishness. This motive is now regularly mentioned in conjunction with other-regarding preferences and fairness in particular. People act out of reciprocity if they respond to acts that they perceive as kind in a kind manner [or hostile to an unkind manner] even though there is not necessarily a future pecuniary gain tied to this action. Typically, in an ultimatum game, responders would be able to "punish" a proposer who divides any money amount unfairly by rejecting the offer. With responder competition however, such punishment is no longer possible. The conclusion can be drawn that competition does not allow people to express their other-regarding preferences, even if they may have them. People may not be purely self-interested, they just don't have the chance to be otherwise.

However, even this conclusion has been rejected by another set of experiment, the gift-exchange game (GEG), initiated by Fehr, Kirchsteiger and Riedl [1993]. The GEG has been used to test, in particular, the efficient wage hypothesis introduced by Akerlof [1982] and Akerlof and Yellen [1990], which says that employers are willing to pay a wage greater than the efficient wage to induce

3. Note that Fehr and co-authors typically talk about self-interest in their papers, while what they actually mean is simply selfishness. We will stick here to the term "selfish" or "pure self-interest" to differentiate it from a more general self-interest that may include other-regarding aspects.

higher effort in the employee. The result of this is involuntary unemployment. However, GEG can also be applied to fair pricing strategies of goods – the higher the offered price, the higher will supposedly be the corresponding quality of a good. The GEG consists of two stages. The first stage is a one-sided oral auction in which employers (buyers) announce their wage-offer (price). Workers (sellers) can accept this offer or not. A particular feature of that experiment is that there are more workers than employers, which creates competition on the offer-side (demand-side) of the market. In the second stage of this experiment, workers (sellers) choose their effort level (quality). Employers and workers are kept in two different rooms, their identity is thus kept secret and they only make anonymous offers. This was particularly to avoid any reputation effect.

The pure self-interest model would predict that workers had no incentive to provide a higher than minimal effort. Knowing this, employers would have no incentive to make a wage offer higher than the market-clearing wage. This implies that the whole surplus would go to the employer. However, the reciprocity hypothesis that Fehr, Kirchsteiger and Riedl wanted to test suggested that there is a positive wage-effort relationship. Employers want to motivate workers to deliver a higher effort and are therefore willing to make a higher wage offer. Workers observe these higher offers and reciprocate by putting in a higher effort. And this is indeed what happened. On average, employers gave workers 42 percent of their surplus even though there were more workers than jobs, which under standard assumptions should have driven wage offers down to the market-clearing level. The average effort of the workers was also four times higher than that predicted by the standard theory. Hence, Fehr *et alii* discovered a clear wage-effort relationship, which moreover tended to persist and did not converge to the market-clearing level even with several repetitions of the game.

In a later paper, Fehr, together with Kirchler, Weichbold and Gächter [1998], criticised the Fehr *et alii* [1993] paper by saying that this experimental design did not allow one to determine whether the high wages were above the competitive level for reciprocity reasons or whether they were high simply because employers expected workers to reject low wage offers [as may happen in an ultimatum game]. They therefore re-conducted this kind of experiment by introducing some further treatments to test this difference. In addition to a GEG treatment, in which labour contracts are notoriously incomplete because the effort cannot be specified in those contracts, they introduce a treatment in which the incompleteness of contracts was eliminated. This is the complete contract market treatment (CCM). In this treatment, the effort-determination stage was removed; effort was set exogenously. This meant that there was no possibility to reciprocate for workers in the case where the employer offered a higher wage. Their hypothesis was that if wages were systematically higher in GEG than in CCM, this would indicate that reciprocal behaviour affects wages. Finally, they also run a bilateral gift exchange (BGE) experiment, in which they remove the competitive factor. This means that there was an equal number of employers and of workers. If wages in BGE were higher than wages in GEG, the conclusion can be drawn that competition does have an effect on wages.

The results show first that in both, the GEG and the BGE treatment, there was a positive-sloped effort-wage relation, indicating that workers made reciprocal effort choices, which is a result that goes against the self-interest interpretation of the economic agent. Second, the average wages were significantly lower in CCM than in either BGE or GEG. From this Fehr *et alii* [1998] draw the conclusion that GEG represents a noncompetitive outcome. Hence employers in the GEG voluntarily pay noncompetitive wages rather than doing so as the best strategy to make sure the offer will be accepted. Finally, they find that the wage-depressing effect of competition is only temporary. Indeed, each treatment was repeated 10 times. One could observe that from period 5 onwards, the wage offers in BGE and GEG tended to be the same and that competitive forces had only an impact in the first few rounds of repetition with wages being lower in GEG than in BGE. Overall they conclude that because such reciprocal behaviour can only be a one-shot phenomenon in the context of this experiment and not the product of reputation or other repeated-game effects, reciprocity is indeed a "preference phenomenon" [p. 344]. These preferences can actually be of two types, as spelt out in particular by Charness [2004]. Either workers are driven by a gain-sharing motive, which means that they want to share their additional income with the employer and therefore deliver more effort [distributional concerns], or they reward good intentions with higher effort and punish bad intentions with lower effort (reciprocity). Employers, on the other hand, deliberately overcompensate workers in order to elicit reciprocal behaviour, which pays off because it generates higher profits. This type of implicit contract is therefore typically one in which employers appeal to the fairness of the worker. By proposing this wage, they "trust" workers to reciprocate. Even though it pays employers to offer higher wages because *in fine* they have a higher profit, the standard pure self-interest model would give employers no reason to "trust" employees since the latter have no binding commitment. Trust here means that employers cannot enforce a particular effort level of the worker. The contract is in that sense incomplete. Indeed, it is this incompleteness of contracts and its consequent non-enforceability that, according to Fehr *et alii* [1993] and Fehr *et alii* [1998], allow for fair and reciprocal behaviour to emerge despite competition. Hence competition allows for other-regarding preferences if contracts are incomplete.

John List [2006] has taken the gift exchange game and brought it into the field. He analyses fairness or social preferences as he calls it in the context of a sports card market. In such a market, buyers approach sports card sellers, who can be both, local and nonlocal dealers, offer a price for a particular quality card they want to purchase and the seller then provides them with a card, whose quality can be assessed by an official grading agency. List conducted several treatments, starting with a standard laboratory experiment in which any reference to "real" markets was removed. He then gradually increased the realism of the transactions. He does so by first adding references to real goods, in this case sports cards, and then letting the participants play the role they would also play in the real world until he eventually moved out of the laboratory into the field where only buyers would be paid subjects who participate in the experiment, but sellers (whose behaviour are the real focus of the experiment) are unaware that they are part of an experiment. Furthermore, he has a treatment in which no sports card are traded but rather, tickets and ticket stubs. In this treatment, no official grading agency was available at first to certify the quality of the ticket, whilst in a later repetition of the experiment, such a grading agency had just been established. These treatments were necessary to investigate how much the influence of the availability of a third party verification and/or reputation would matter in the determination of the sellers' behaviour. The results are remarkable. While in the laboratory context, List's experiment could replicate the behaviour found in previous GEGs, that is a positive price-quality relationship indicating reciprocal behaviour or the existence of social preferences [although there is a slightly decreasing price-quality relationship with more context], in the market environment, social preferences generally do not have a major impact. That is, if third-party verification is available, the behaviour of local dealers was consistent with both, the gift exchange and the pure self-interest model, while non-local dealers' behaviour was in line with the pure self-interest theory only. When no third-party verification was available, the sellers' behaviour was consonant only with a standard money-maximising theory. This implies that if there is a positive price-quality relationship, this stems purely from reputational concerns (what we referred to as "strategic nobility" in the second section and which thus is perfectly compatible with purely self-interested behaviour). Hence contrary to the Fehr and co-authors' [1993, 1998] conclusion that competition with incompleteness of contracts allows for reciprocal behaviour, List shows that this is not the case. In particular if there is no third-party verification, hence if contracts are not enforceable, sellers behave in a selfish manner.

We have therefore seen that it is not competition per se that drives out other-regarding or reciprocal behaviour. One suggestion was that the existence of incomplete contracts and its non-enforceability might leave the door open for such behaviour. But we have again seen that by moving from the laboratory into the field, even this avenue seems to be barred. So what happens as we move from the laboratory to the field that makes other-regarding preferences disappear? One clear difference between the lab experiment reviewed in the previous section and List's field experiment is that in the latter, sellers really earn their money, whilst in the laboratory experiments, subjects have only to deal with windfall money. Another aspect is that in none of those experiments, do subjects exert any real effort, but rather choose between contracts with different effort levels. But earned money and effort may be important variables that explain human behaviour.

There is now a small set of experiments that shows that when subjects earn their money, this has an important influence on behaviour. Cherry *et alii* [2002] for example show that when subjects earn money from solving a quiz prior to the distribution phase in a dictator game (where, contrary to an ultimatum game, responders are only receivers of the money and no longer have the right to decide whether to accept of to reject the offer), other-regarding behaviour was greatly diminished in comparison to the situation in which they receive windfall money. This finding has been repeated in a dictator game experiment conducted by Oxoby and Spraggon [2008] where dictators were paid according to their performance on a 20 questions exam taken from a Canadian Management Admissions Test. Hoffman *et alii* [1994] show that when participants earned the right to be the proposer in an ultimatum game based on the performance in a knowledge test, the median offer drops relative to the situation in which the right is randomly allocated. Gneezy and List [2006] conducted a GEG in the field where they paid subjects to perform a particular task. One task was to computerise the holdings of a small library at the university, another a door-to-door fundraising campaign to support the Natural Hazards Mitigation Reserach Centre at a large university. They conducted two treatments by dividing subjects into two groups. In the *noGift* treatment, a group earned 12 dollars for the library task and 10 dollars per hour for the fundraising task, exactly as announced during the recruitment campaign. In the *Gift* treatment, a group of subjects were informed that instead of the 10 (12) dollars it was announced they could earn, they would earn

20 dollars per hour. For the library task, subjects were hired for about 6 hours, in the fundraising task subjects participated during one single weekend. Reciprocal behaviour did have an effect – but only in the first few hours of each task. Any increased effort wanes quickly and the effort in both treatments became statistically insignificant. Gneezy and List attribute this to the effect of *duration*, which incites people to change their reference point over time and thus to change their behaviour. Our interpretation would be that whilst at the beginning, subjects feel somehow obliged to provide more effort because they are offered a higher wage, the "earned money effect" kicks in quickly and reduces their effort. Hence real effort for which one earns money seems to dampen other-regarding behaviour. This of course is simply our hypothesis, as we are not aware of any experiment that has tested specifically the earned money effect in GEGs.

Can we therefore conclude that for other-regarding behaviour to exist subjects need to redistribute windfall money rather than earned money? Not quite. Oxoby and Spraggon [2008] show that if the receivers earn the money that the dictators have to redistribute, generally, dictators respect the invested effort of the receivers and give more in comparison to standard dictator games. It is also true that the receivers must trust dictators to redistribute the money and not to keep it especially in those cases in which the receivers invest more than a minimum effort. Cherry and Shogren [2008] show that the earned money effect is attenuated when dictators are informed about whether receivers had no opportunity to earn money other than through their allocation or whether they did have the opportunity but did not take it up. The result shows that whether dictators' money was earned or not, they offered more to recipients that had no opportunity to earn or receive money, and offered less to those that opted out of this opportunity. Hence in both types of experiments, other-regarding or social preferences are not ruled out with earned money, but they have much less importance. Generally, other regarding preferences seem to be stronger in those cases where the receiver has had no responsibility for not earning any extra money versus those that had one insofar as they rejected the possibility to earn some extra money.

In summary, these last few experiments clearly tell us that effort is a variable that is taken seriously by most people, whether as a factor that authorises a person to give less because she previously had to spend effort to earn that money, or whether as a factor that induces a person to redistribute towards the person who undertook the effort. Moreover, people are willing to redistribute towards those who are in need even with earned money, but feel less strongly about it when people are held responsible for the need in which they find themselves. This conclusion goes hand in hand with findings of a recent large scale experiment that tested whether people's preferences for redistribution, depending on how they earned their money, coincided with existing theories of justice on the subject of equality of opportunity [Chanel *et alii* 2009]. In this experiment, subjects had the chance to earn money through four different channels, commonly discussed in the equality of opportunity literature, namely effort, social circumstances (*e.g.* some people receive an important inheritance, others don't), option luck (luck that was voluntarily chosen such as participating at a lottery) and brute luck (events that affected a person independently of their doing, such as a natural catastrophe). It turns out that people tend to redistribute for social circumstances and for brute luck, but not for effort and option luck. The latter are two variables for which people can be held responsible, whilst the first two are independent of a person's doing. As the authors show, this conforms particularly well with Ronald Dworkin's [1981] view of equality of opportunity.

Given the evidence cited above, one may wonder whether a market economy makes people cherish effort and with it responsiblity and that it is those two variables that eventually determine the willingness to redistribute. This would mean that the market forges certain values that indirectly influence people's other-regarding behaviour or preferences. Before markets became such a prominent institution, aristocratic and feudal systems reigned and may have promulgated other values. Under these regimes, it could be argued that social circumstances are favoured over effort. As with the caste system in India, those who are valued are those who were born into the right "social position" and not those who had made a greater effort. They lived off "rents" often taken on the back of other people's labour, that had nothing to do with their own "input" into the production process. But again, we do not have strong evidence for this conclusion, namely that the market system fosters certain values that then determine people's other-regarding. This hypothesis has not yet experimentally been tested. Conducting further experiments would certainly be a step forward in analysing whether the market as an institutions fosters particular "kinds" of individuals.

Before we conclude, we should also consider the following experiment. Jacquemet *et alii* [2009] set up a Vickrey second price auction with a prior earned money phase. Despite the fact that for this kind of auction, the best strategy is to reveal the truth, *i.e.* one's true evaluation of the object, it has been observed that with windfall money, people bid insincerely, especially off the-margins bidders. Jacquemet *et alii* [2009] state that this kind of experiment helps to distinguish an important point. Referring also to experiments mentioned in previous paragraphs in which the earned money effect reduces a dictator's willingness to share money with the receiver, they say that it is not clear whether this is the result of social preferences becoming less important or whether earning money helps to sharpen people's minds and to become more focused on the selfish, and in this sense, more rational, outcome. The second price Vickrey auction is helpful for this since it is a purely "private" mechanism, and no social preferences can come into play. Hence if earned money changes anything in the bidding strategies of subjects, this must be because earned money makes people more rational in the usual sense. They observe that indeed, with an earned money phase, people engage in more sincere bidding.

This experiment thus shows that after all, other-regarding preferences seem to have much less impact than previously thought and that the earned money mechanisms makes people more focused on their pure self-interest, and in standard theory more rational behaviour. Of course, in the context of a second price Vickrey auction, it is clear what the most rational strategy is. In this sense it is easy to refer to any other strategy as irrational. However, in the context of social preferences, this is less clear because other-regarding preferences per se do not need to be irrational. But not everybody would agree with this view.

4. Concluding remarks

In this paper, we have given some arguments in favour of the view that the economic agent has more than one motivation and that it should be regarded as consistent with rationality to act on the basis of such motivations. Kenneth Binmore [2006] on the other hand thinks that the self-interested model is perfectly satisfactory and that no other motivation needs to be introduced. This does not exclude the idea that people can act in an other-regarding ways. Indeed, he thinks that cultural evolution has made us human beings accept certain social norms that favour cooperation:

> Since everyone in an ancestral hunter-gatherer group would have been a relative of some kind, it is therefore not surprising that most of us seem to be wired up to be willing to make *small* sacrifices to help out total strangers. Some of us are occasionally willing to make *big* sacrifices, but only a tiny fraction of saints are willing to do so on a regular basis. [p. 83]

Binmore therefore thinks that the current discussion, led by behavioural economists, who insist that a large fraction of individuals have other-regarding preferences, is vastly exaggerated[4]. He insists that the predictions of standard game theory works fairly well most of the time if the problem in laboratory experiments are presented in a non-complex, user-friendly style, subjects are given

4. In fact, Fehr and Schmidt [1999] "notoriously" found a ratio of 40: 60, the former indicating the percentage of those with other-regarding preferences in a population, the latter those with self-interest only. We say "notoriously" because this ratio has incited Binmore and Shaked [2010] to write an extensive critique on the way this has been calculated. Fehr and Schmidt's [2010] reply is also interesting to read in this context but it does not fully address Binmore and Shaked's critiques.

adequate incentives and they have ample time for trial-and-error learning. Other-regarding preferences would then, in the long run, be ruled out. Binmore's view therefore suggest that markets as such do not have a particular influence on human behaviour. Given evolutionary forces, natural selection processes have acted on "us" over much period, starting even before mankind was living as a hunter-gatherer society. In that sense, the market's influence only represents a tiny fraction of the whole evolutionary history.

It is difficult to determine the right answer to this difficult question and it certainly requires further investigation. Clearly, evolutionary and "one-shot" forces may be at play at the same time and it may be ridiculous to try to find clear-cut answers. Hence, bearing Binmore and Jacquemet *et alii* experiment in mind, let us summarise the main arguments of this paper. In section 2, we have seen that it is wrong to say that the economic agent is "by nature" selfish. We think that this is fair to say even from an evolutionary perspective because it may need at least some errors and trials to determine that the self-interested strategy is the best one to apply. Economic theory is not restricted to a selfish individual. But if the individual is not purely self-interested then what economic theory would need to investigate further are the consequences on the measurement of wellbeing. Furthermore, if the economic agent is not purely self-interested by nature, then something has led him to behave in this way. This is the question that we dealt with primarily in this article. We investigated whether the market as such has anything to do with making the individual more selfish. We have considered here, in particular, the influence of competition, perfect contracts and earning money. In all those cases, and under particular circumstances, we have seen that these factors reduce other-regarding behaviour. Two particular issues seem to be noteworthy. One is that, contrary to the rather widespread view that it is the incompleteness of contracts that allows for social norms and other-regarding behaviour to emerge, List's experiment shows that incompleteness of contracts and its corresponding non-enforceability fosters pure self-interest. The second point to note is that if it is primarily the earned money factor that reduces other-regarding behaviour then this may be attributed to the market economy, in the following sense. People earned their resources before the emergence of markets, but it was only when goods came to be exchanged either by barter or for money that the considerations that we have evoked became important. Thus the relative value of goods might be determined by effort in a market economy, a sort of early labour theory of value. This would be in contrast to previous times (or other actual social institutions, such as the family) and it may be that for this reason effort and the corresponding responsibility factor that influences people's behaviour make "self-centred interest" more salient in the market context than other interests the person may have.

The next question is whether it is, in fact, correct that effort and responsibility have achieved such an importance in market economies. This kind of interrogation brings us of course to the core of justice debates. Indeed, it is, for example, Marc Fleurbaey's view [2001] that responsibility is a particular value-judgement but that it should not be given so much weight as to allow major inequalities to emerge. This complements our hypothesis that it is the market system that forges some values that then determine how much selfishness and how much other-regarding behaviour can be observed. But other values may (and probably should) also emerge. This is especially true in a world in which sustainable development, climate change and global justice and the idea of global public goods are widely discussed. How this will or should influence people's behaviour will need to be investigated. But, in such a context, the purely self-interested agent may become less plausible as a basic assumption.

REFERENCES

AKERLOF G.A. 1982, "Labor Contracts as Partial Gift Exchange", *Quarterly Journal of Economics*, vol. XCVII, p. 543-569.

— and YELLEN J.L., 1990, "The Fair Wage-Effort Hypothesis and Unemployment", *Quarterly Journal of Economics*, vol. CV, p. 255-283.

— and KRANTON R., 2000, "Economics and Identity", *Quaterly Journal of Economics*, vol. 65, n° 3, p. 715-753.

ANDREONI J. and MILLER J., 2002, "Giving According to GARP: An Experimental Test of the Consistency of Preferences for Altruism", *Econometrica*, vol. 70, n° 2, p. 737-753.

BINMORE K., 2006, "Why do people cooperate?", *Politics, Philosophy and Economics*, vol. 5, p. 81-96.

– 2009, *Rational Decisions*, Princeton, Princeton University Press.

— and SHAKED A., 2010, "Experimental economics: where next?", *Journal of Economic Behavior and Organization*, vol. 73, n° 1, p. 87-100.

BOWLES S., 1998, "Endogenous Preferences pp. The Cultural Consequences of Markets and Other Economic Institutions", *Journal of Economic Literature*, vol. 36, n° 1, p. 75-111.

BROOME J., 1999, *Ethics out of Economics*, Cambridge, Cambridge University Press.

BRUNI L. and SUGDEN R., 2008, "Fraternity: Why the Market Need To Be a Morally Free Zone", *Economics and Philosophy*, vol. 24, p. 35-64.

CAMERER C., 2003, *Behavioral Game Theory*, Princeton, Princeton University Press.

CHANEL O., LU I., LUCHINI S., TESCHL M. and TRANNOY A., 2009, "Experimental Distributive Justice: How We Earn Money Matters", GREQAM *Working Paper.*

CHARNESS G., 2004, "Attribution and Reciprocity in an Experimental Labor Market", *Journal of Labor Economics*, vol. 22, p. 665-688.

CHERRY T.L., FRYKBLOM P. and SHOGREN J., 2002, "Hardnose the dictator", *American Economic Review*, vol. 92, n° 4, p. 1218-1221.

— and SHOGREN J., 2008, "Self-interest, sympathy and the origin of endowments", *Economics Letters*, vol. 101, p. 69-72.

DAVIS D. and HOLT Ch., 1993, *Experimental Economics*, Princeton, Princeton University Press.

DWORKIN R., 1981, "What is equality? Part 1: Equality of welfare, Part 2: Equality of resources", *Philosophy and Public Affairs*, vol. 10, p. 185-246 and p. 283-345.

EDGEWORTH F.Y., 1881, *Mathematical Psychics*, London, Kegan Paul.

FEHR E. and FISCHBACHER U., 2002, "Why Social Preferences Matter – The Impact of Non-Selfish Motives on Competition, Cooperation and Incentives", *The Economic Journal*, vol. 112, n° 478, p. C1-C33.

— KIRCHLER E., WEICHBOLD A. and GÄCHTER S., 1998, "When Social Norms Overpower Competition: Gift Exchange in Experimental Labor Markets", *Journal of Labor Economics*, vol. 16, n° 2, p. 324-351.

— KIRCHSTEIGER G. and RIEDL A., 1993, "Does Fairness prevent Market Clearing? An Experimental Investigation", *Quarterly Journal of Economics*, vol. CVIII, p. 437-460.

— and SCHMIDT K., 1999, "A Theory of Fairness, Competition, and Cooperation", *Quarterly Journal of Economics*, vol. 114, n° 3, p. 817-868.

— 2010, "On inequity aversion: A reply to Binmore and Shaked", *Journal of Economic Organization and Behavior*, vol. 73, n° 1, p. 101-108.

FISCHBACHER U., FONG Ch. and FEHR E., 2009. "Fairness, errors and the power of competition", *Journal of Economic Behavior and Organization*, vol. 72, n° 1, p. 527-545.

FLEURBAEY M., 2001, "Egalitarian Opportunities", *Law and Philosophy*, vol. 20, p. 499-530.

FREY B. and MEIER S., 2004, "Social Comparisons and Pro-Social Behavior pp. Testing Conditional Cooperation in a Field Experiment", *American Economic Review*, vol. 94, n° 5, p. 1717-1722.

GAUTHIER D., 1986, *Morals by Agreement*, Oxford, Oxford University Press.

GNEEZY U. and LIST J., 2006, "Putting Behavioral Economics to Work: Testing for Gift Exchange in Labor markets Using Field Experiments", *Econometrica*, vol. 74, n° 5, p. 1365-1384.

HENRICH J., BOYD R., Bowles S., CAMERER C., FEHR E., GINTIS H. *et alii*, 2005, "'Economic man' in cross-cultural perspective: Behavioral experiments in 15 small-scale societies", *Behavioral and Brain Sciences*, vol. 28, p. 795-815.

HOFFMAN E., MCCABE K. and SMITH V., 1994, "Preferences, property rights, and anonymity in bargaining games", *Games and Economic Behavior*, vol. 7, p. 346-380.

JACQUEMET N., JOULE R.-V., LUCHINI S. and SHOGREN J., 2009, "Earned wealth, engaged bidders? Evidence from a second-price auction", *Economics Letters*, vol. 105, n° 1, p. 36-38.

LEDYARD J.O., 1995, "Public Goods pp. A Survey of Experimental Research", *in* J. Kagel and R. Alvin, *Handbook of Experimental Economics*, Princeton, Princeton University Press, p. 111-194.

LIST J., 2006, "The Behavioralist Meets the Market: Measuring Social Preferences and Reputation Effects in Actual Transactions", *Journal of Political Economy*, vol. 114, n° 1, p. 1-37.

MEIER S., 2007, "A Survey of Economic Theories and Field Evidence on Pro-Social Behavior", *in* B. Frey and A. Stutzer, *Economics and Psychology: A Promising New Cross-Disciplinary Field*, Cambridge (Mass.), MIT Press, p. 51-88.

OXOBY R.J. and SPRAGGON J., 2008, "Mine and Yours: Property Rights in Dictator Games", *Journal of Economic Behavior and Organization*, vol. 65, n° 3-4, p. 703-713.

ROBBINS L., 1984 [1935], " An Essay on the Scope and Nature of Economic Science", *in* D. Hausman, *The Philosophy of Economics: An Anthology*, Cambridge, Cambridge University Press.

ROTH A.E., PRASNIKAR V., OKUNO-FUJIWARA M. and ZAMIR S., 1991, "Bargaining and market behaivor in Jerusalem, Ljubljana, Pittsburg, and Tokyo: an experimental investigation", *American Economic Review*, vol. 81, n° 5, p. 1068-1095.

SEN A., 1973, "Behaviour and the Concept of Preference", *Economica*, 40, n° 159, p. 241-259.

– 1977, "Rational Fools: A Critique of the Behavioral Foundations of Economic Theory", *Philosophy and Public Affairs*, vol. 6, n° 4, p. 317-344.

– 1985, "Goals, Commitment and Identity", *Journal of Law, Economics and Organization*, vol. 1, n° 2, p. 341-355.

– 1997, "Maximization and the Act of Choice", *Econometrica*, vol. 65, n° 4, p. 745-779.

– 1999, *Development as Freedom*, Oxford, Oxford University Press.

– 2002, *Rationality and Freedom*, Cambridge (Mass.), Harvard University Press.

SMITH V.L., 1962, "An Experimental Study of Competitive Market Behavior", *Journal of Political Economy*, vol. 70, p. 111-137.

SOBEL J., 2009, "Generous actors, selfish actions: markets with other-regarding preferences", *International Review of Economics*, vol. 56, p. 3-16.

ACHEVÉ D'IMPRIMER
EN AOÛT 2010
PAR L'IMPRIMERIE
DE LA MANUTENTION
A MAYENNE
FRANCE
N° 10N-86

Dépôt légal : 3e trimestre 2010

BULLETIN D'ABONNEMENT

Revue de Philosophie Économique

Je soussigné(e), M./Mme

Nom : .... Prénom : ....

Institution : .... N° TVA : ....

Rue : .... Numéro : ....

C.P. : .... Ville : .... Pays : ....

commande :

au prix de 50 euros TTC (frais de port inclus) pour la France et de 55 euros TTC (frais de port inclus) pour l'étranger

.... abonnement(s) annuel 2010 à la *Revue de Philosophie Économique* (deux numéros par an).

au prix de 30 euros TTC (frais de port en sus)

.... ex. du numéro 2, vol. 10, décembre 2009, 978-2-7116-5201-3

.... ex. du numéro 1, vol. 10, juillet 2009, *Enjeux éthiques en économie de la santé*, 978-2-7116-5200-6

.... ex. du numéro 2, vol. 9, décembre 2008, 978-2-7117-3511-2

.... ex. du numéro 1, vol. 9, juillet 2008, *Démocratie d'entreprise*, 978-2-7117-3510-5

.... ex. du numéro 14, 2006/2, 978-2-7117-3507-5

.... ex. du numéro 13, 2006/1, 978-2-7117-3506-8

.... ex. du numéro 9, 2004/1, *Le concept d'identité*, 978-2-7117-3502-0

.... ex. du numéro 8, 2003/2, 978-2-7117-3501-3

.... ex. du numéro 7, 2003/1, *Autour de John Rawls*, 978-2-7117-3500-6

Paiement :

❐ par chèque vancaire à l'ordre de « Librairie Philosophique J. Vrin » (joindre le chèque au bulletin d'abonnement)

❐ par règlement administratif (joindre le bon de commande au bulletin d'abonnement)

Date : .... Signature

À renvoyer à : Librairie Philosophique J. Vrin
À l'attention de Frédéric Mendès – fmendes@vrin.fr
6 place de la Sorbonne
75005 Paris – France